A Practical Guide to Mergers and Acquisitions:

Truth is Stranger than Fiction

Louis M. Richard

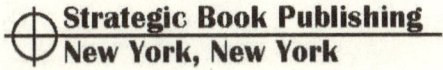
Strategic Book Publishing
New York, New York

Copyright © 2008

All rights reserved – by Louis M Richard

No part of this book may be reproduced or transmitted in any form or by any means, graphic, electronic, or mechanical, including photocopying, recording, taping, or by any information storage retrieval system, without the permission, in writing, from the publisher.

Strategic Book Publishing
An imprint of Writers Literary & Publishing Services, Inc.
845 Third Avenue, 6th Floor – 6016
New York, NY 10022
www.strategicbookpublishing.com

ISBN: 978-1-934925-83-6/SKU 1-934925-83-7

Printed in the United States of America

Table of Contents

Preface 1
Introduction 3
Chapter 1: Why Do Companies Make Acquisitions? 9
    Digression #1 The Toothpaste Man 11
Chapter 2: An Acquirer's Tool Bag 15
    Target Templates 15
    Sector Surveys 16
    Comparables and Valuation Models 17
    Digression #2 Honest John (HJ) 20
Chapter 3: Why Do Most Acquisitions Fail? 26
    Culture 26
    Integration 27
    Change 28
    Attitude 29
    PTM Reflux 30
    Intentional Fraud 30
    Getting it Wrong 31
    Digression #3 Adventures in Paradise? 32
Chapter 4: Why Are Companies Sold? 35
    Distressed Sellers 35
    Life Cycle Venders 36
    Spin-Offs and Strategic Sales 37
    Habitual Sellers/Serial Entrepreneurs 38
    Digression #4 Luck of the Irish 40
Chapter 5: Buy-Side Transactions 44

Methodology	44
Buy-Side Collateral	45
Mandate from the Top	47
Commitment and Determination	48
Vision or Utility	50
But have they?	51
Strategy	52
Pace	54
Arguments for slow pace include:	54
Fast-paced processes on the other hand drive better outcomes.	55
Attitude	56
Digression #5 Wise Man	57
Chapter 6: Sell-Side Transactions	**63**
Methodology	63
Reasons for Sale	63
Relentless Searches for the Premium Buyer	64
Competitive Tension	66
Relationships, Brand, and Quality	67
Strategic Fits	68
Valuations—Art and Science	70
Pace	72
Sales Collateral	73
Confidentiality	74
Renegade Buyers	75
Digression #6 The Banker	76
Chapter 7: Raising Capital In Australia	**80**

Methodology	44
Buy-Side Collateral	45
Mandate from the Top	47
Commitment and Determination	48
Vision or Utility	50
But have they?	51
Strategy	52
Pace	54
Arguments for slow pace include:	54
Fast-paced processes on the other hand drive better outcomes.	55
Attitude	56
Digression #5 Wise Man	57
Chapter 6: Sell-Side Transactions	**63**
Methodology	63
Reasons for Sale	63
Relentless Searches for the Premium Buyer	64
Competitive Tension	66
Relationships, Brand, and Quality	67
Strategic Fits	68
Valuations—Art and Science	70
Pace	72
Sales Collateral	73
Confidentiality	74
Renegade Buyers	75
Digression #6 The Banker	76
Chapter 7: Raising Capital In Australia	**80**

Table of Contents

Preface 1
Introduction 3
Chapter 1: Why Do Companies Make Acquisitions? 9
    Digression #1 The Toothpaste Man 11
Chapter 2: An Acquirer's Tool Bag 15
    Target Templates 15
    Sector Surveys 16
    Comparables and Valuation Models 17
    Digression #2 Honest John (HJ) 20
Chapter 3: Why Do Most Acquisitions Fail? 26
    Culture 26
    Integration 27
    Change 28
    Attitude 29
    PTM Reflux 30
    Intentional Fraud 30
    Getting it Wrong 31
    Digression #3 Adventures in Paradise? 32
Chapter 4: Why Are Companies Sold? 35
    Distressed Sellers 35
    Life Cycle Venders 36
    Spin-Offs and Strategic Sales 37
    Habitual Sellers/Serial Entrepreneurs 38
    Digression #4 Luck of the Irish 40
Chapter 5: Buy-Side Transactions 44

Chapter 8: Miscellaneous Trivia & Minutiae 86
    Advisors 86
    Advisory Fees 89
    Management Meetings 92
    Term Sheets 93
    Teasers 96
    Contacts 96
    Non-Binding Offers 98
    Best and Final Offers (BAFOs) 98
    Process and Schedule for Transaction 99
    Assessment of Bids 100
        Certainty of Completion 100
        Speed of Completion 101
        Transaction Structure 102
        Transaction Balance Sheet 102
        Consideration Payable 102
        Other Factors 105
    Digression #7 Finglish 107
Chapter 9: I Told You So 111
About the Author 113

Preface

This text began as yet another set of notes to accompany Newport Capital's engagement methodologies, for use by Newport's professional staff. I have a preoccupation with business processes and methodologies, in a professional services context. As the text expanded, I decided to lighten things up with some diversions to possibly lighten the reader's load in digesting what otherwise could be considered somewhat dry fare.

As I continued with the text, anxious to comprehensively cover key aspects of the methodologies, it assumed a life of its own. It occurred to me that I hadn't encountered a practical guide to execution of M&A transactions, so I altered the shape of the text to provide a useful handbook for M&A practitioners. I would have appreciated such a handbook when I began learning the craft of M&A transaction execution—back in the mists of time.

It also occurred to me, as I progressed to the final draft, that the text disclosed processes and methodologies that I consider to be my and Newport's intellectual property. Worse still, it occurred to me that business owners could choose to use the text as a guide to rolling their own transactions. Of course, the reality is that a cookbook doesn't create great chefs. Reading the processes and methodologies is one thing; expertly executing complex, sensitive, critically important business transactions is another matter. I have read books on human anatomy and I haven't yet attempted surgery.

I hope readers find the text informative and useful and will be pleased to receive comments and suggestions for inclusion in a planned update. I also hope that readers find the diversions utterly unbelievable but somewhat amusing. Regrettably, the diversions are factual—truth is indeed stranger that fiction. The real fascination of the M&A practitioner's craft is not the stress, money, or exacting nature of the process, but rather the extraordinary nature of the people you encounter along the way.

Balmoral,
March 2008

Introduction

I entered the ICT industry in the early 1960s when I left my job teaching to join IBM Australia. For reasons I can't adequately explain, much of my career, spent either as an executive in large companies or as an entrepreneur building my own hopes and dreams, M&A was part of my DNA. I know of no relevant family history—most of my forebears died happy and relatively sane.

At Computer Resources Company—a truly great Australian ICT enterprise of the 1960s, '70s, and '80s—which I ran for three years as CEO—M&A became part of my daily fare. I also had the great pleasure, and pain, of launching some successful start-ups, including a leasing company that competed with Allco in Allco's early days. We acquired and divested regularly, mostly with good results. We buried our few mistakes, and the tax commissioner shared our pain on write-offs. Of course, in those days, capital gains tax was non-existent, and the prospects of building a business with a view to an exit was all the more enticing. I attempted an MBO, in league with my future partner in ATAC Group, George Farley. Malcolm Irving at Martin Corporation acted as our advisor, but the deal failed when the transaction balance sheet was produced—too few assets included in the transaction, and too many liabilities.

At ATAC, my partner George Farley and I formed various joint ventures, including a joint venture with Adriatic, Bishopsgate, and Consolidated insurance companies, and another joint venture with New Zealand's Fletcher Challenge group. Start-ups were also a feature of ATAC, most of which worked and grew. One such was a start-up to act as the MasterCard International agent for Australia, after a bust-up between Visa, MasterCard, and the Big Banks. The MasterCard applications would—if run on ATAC's IBM-equipped bureau—have taken months to process a days worth of trading. So my inestimably smart partner and his team managed to write the entire system for an Altos micro, which took about six weeks to implement and ran without a single failure. To pay the merchants, I used to call MasterCard US and quote the maiden name of the CEO's (Australian) wife. MasterCard then transferred the required millions to our account—an early example of good governance.

After my return from working in London in 1986, I worked on a long-term contract as general manager, business development, of Computer Power Group. In this capacity, I worked closely with the team and on occasion with the founder/entrepreneur extraordinaire Roger Allen. My colleagues started calling me Mr. Bond as most of the M&A opportunities came across my desk. Roger Allen would, on occasion, pass my desk and leave a deposit (of papers) related to an idea or deal he had been incubating. One such deposit led to the formation of a major joint venture with the then Overseas Telecommunications Commission (OTC), which was passionately driven by George Maltby. The joint venture, which I ran for the period of winning a major deal for outsourcing of the NSW government's telecommunications network, pranged when the OTC was merged with Telstra. Premier Greiner was not a Telstra admirer.

In the late 1980s, as a result of selling the Computer Power PC and maintenance business to ICL—the British firm—I became ICL's Asia Pacific one-man M&A team. The ride was furious and ICL acquired nine engineering operations in twelve months. Unfortunately, I found the ICL Australian ecosystem quite toxic. Those that weren't there for a tour of ICL's global franchises, then back home, had been banished to the colony for bad behavior, and got up to considerable non-productive mischief. My poor boss, Robert L Kaye, hovered near suicide due to constant and unexpected bombs lobbed into his vicinity by various miscreants. While on a visit to ICL headquarters at Putney Bridge, I got wind of the impending purchase of various ICL companies by Fujitsu.

I returned home, resigned, then mounted a bid for ICL to defeat the Fujitsu bid. John Button, the responsible minister, and his advisor Trevor Robinson (both recently departed from this coil for better things) helped out and several large corporates were encouraged to back our bid of about AU$1.5 billion. Unfortunately, IBM got wind of our gig and very effectively torpedoed it. A real pity, as ICL would have given Australian ICT used to call MasterCard US and quote the maiden name of the CEO's (Australian) wife. MasterCard then transferred the required millions to our account—an early example of good governance.

After my return from working in London in 1986, I worked on a long-term contract as general manager, business development, of Computer Power Group. In this capacity, I worked closely with the team and on occasion with the founder/entrepreneur extraordinaire Roger Allen. My colleagues started calling me Mr. Bond as most of the M&A opportunities came across my desk. Roger Allen would, on occasion, pass my desk and leave a deposit (of papers) related to an idea or deal he had been incubating. One such deposit led to the formation of a major joint venture with the then Overseas Telecommunications Commission (OTC), which was passionately driven by George Maltby. The joint venture, which I ran for the period of winning a major deal for outsourcing of the NSW government's telecommunications network, pranged when the OTC was merged with Telstra. Premier Greiner was not a Telstra admirer.

In the late 1980s, as a result of selling the Computer Power PC and maintenance business to ICL—the British firm—I became ICL's Asia Pacific one-man M&A team. The ride was furious and ICL acquired nine engineering operations in twelve months. Unfortunately, I found the ICL Australian ecosystem quite toxic. Those that weren't there for a tour of ICL's global franchises, then back home, had been banished to the colony for bad behavior, and got up to considerable non-productive mischief. My poor boss, Robert L Kaye, hovered near suicide due to constant and unexpected bombs lobbed into his vicinity by various miscreants. While on a visit to ICL headquarters at Putney Bridge, I got wind of the impending purchase of various ICL companies by Fujitsu.

I returned home, resigned, then mounted a bid for ICL to defeat the Fujitsu bid. John Button, the responsible minister, and his advisor Trevor Robinson (both recently departed from this coil for better things) helped out and several large corporates were encouraged to back our bid of about AU$1.5 billion. Unfortunately, IBM got wind of our gig and very effectively torpedoed it. A real pity, as ICL would have given Australian ICT

Introduction

I entered the ICT industry in the early 1960s when I left my job teaching to join IBM Australia. For reasons I can't adequately explain, much of my career, spent either as an executive in large companies or as an entrepreneur building my own hopes and dreams, M&A was part of my DNA. I know of no relevant family history—most of my forebears died happy and relatively sane.

At Computer Resources Company—a truly great Australian ICT enterprise of the 1960s, '70s, and '80s—which I ran for three years as CEO—M&A became part of my daily fare. I also had the great pleasure, and pain, of launching some successful start-ups, including a leasing company that competed with Allco in Allco's early days. We acquired and divested regularly, mostly with good results. We buried our few mistakes, and the tax commissioner shared our pain on write-offs. Of course, in those days, capital gains tax was non-existent, and the prospects of building a business with a view to an exit was all the more enticing. I attempted an MBO, in league with my future partner in ATAC Group, George Farley. Malcolm Irving at Martin Corporation acted as our advisor, but the deal failed when the transaction balance sheet was produced—too few assets included in the transaction, and too many liabilities.

At ATAC, my partner George Farley and I formed various joint ventures, including a joint venture with Adriatic, Bishopsgate, and Consolidated insurance companies, and another joint venture with New Zealand's Fletcher Challenge group. Start-ups were also a feature of ATAC, most of which worked and grew. One such was a start-up to act as the MasterCard International agent for Australia, after a bust-up between Visa, MasterCard, and the Big Banks. The MasterCard applications would—if run on ATAC's IBM-equipped bureau—have taken months to process a days worth of trading. So my inestimably smart partner and his team managed to write the entire system for an Altos micro, which took about six weeks to implement and ran without a single failure. To pay the merchants, I companies a global platform to promote and distribute Australian-grown intellectual property (IP).

In the wake of the failed attempt to buy ICL for Australia, I decided to start Newport Capital. I had encountered Broadview Associates, a U.S.-based ICT sector M&A leader started by Gil Mintz, the ex-CFO of ADP in the United States. I liked Broadview's model of using ICT sector executives to masquerade as I-bankers, rather I-bankers masquerading as technologists.

My inaugural partner was Gary Walter Jackson, freshly departed from the managing director's office of Microsoft Australia. Gary had somehow embarked on an enterprise importing and selling sky tubes—an up-market, high tech form of skylight. Our fledgling enterprise, operating from the sky tube premises Gary had leased in Atchison Street, St. Leonards, should—in Gary's view—not be constrained by petty factors such as available cash. Gary's own cash was in popular demand by ex-wives, children, mistresses, and Masserati dealers. To remove this annoyance, Gary and I approached the Japan Australia Venture Capital Fund. The fund was then being managed by Dov Brener and Tim James, whom I had met at Computer Power. Dov and Tim were fans of Gary's and to some degree, of mine. Somewhat surprisingly, Gary left after about six months to join Sybase, after Gary and I sold the then locally owned Open Vision Systems (OVS, established by Steve Clark and Mike Burmeister) to Sybase.

The Sybase VPs cornered Gary in a bar in Singapore, and made him an offer he couldn't refuse. Gary's departure caused some angst with Dov and Tim, and to settle the score we billed Sybase a hiring fee for Gary, which was paid. Gary then went on to bigger and better things with CISCO and others, and is now running the Asia Pacific operations for a CISCO competitor headed for NASDAQ.

Hiring opportunistically, mainly by referrals, we rode off enthusiastically into the later 1990s to build the team (at the height of the dot-com and Y2K madness) to thirty-two heads. Alf Stamp (previously a New Zealand soccer star, now chief financial officer of Principle Advisory), Jay Hennock (now building an Internet play—Moveit), Charlie Zoi (ex-group managing director at Telstra and self-proclaimed swordsman extraordinaire), Peter Robson (ex-secretary of the Public Sector Union and close apparatchik with various industry sector fund managers), Stuart Mitchell (now CFO at Ironbridge Capital), Karlis Felzenberg (ex-Needham & Company U.S.), Tim Ebbeck (now CEO at SAP), Ben Cardillo (ex-head of new media at the ABC) and others maintained great passion and helped build the enterprise.

In 2000, Malcolm Irving OAM, whom I had known at Martin Corporation, joined me as chairman of Newport Capital and chairman of our fund management operation. Malcolm and I journeyed relentlessly to Taiwan, for deep and meaningful meetings with our fifty-fifty partners in the fund management operation—China Development Industrial Bank (CDIB), who, I was told, were purchasers of Paul Keating's pig farm, but this was never verified.

The standard agenda in Taipei was a breakfast chat with key players, followed by a formal meeting with ten to twenty participants, all PhD-qualified, all taking notes. They would assure us that they would look into the matters we raised and probably adjourned to the Tangalin Club to enjoy a real meal. Benny Hu, president of CDIB, explained to me that M&A was not a business function in Taiwan. If you wanted to sell, buy, or raise capital, you lunched at the Tangalin Club and transactions were completed over the entrees.

We would be dispatched with a driver (yet again) to the Palace Museum. After an adequate number of visits to the museum, we preferred to ask the driver to take us back to our hotel, and onward to the airport.

Establishment of the two Newport funds in 1999 through 2000, including a Commonwealth-sponsored industry innovation fund (IIF), and the subsequent rigors—nearly rigor mortis—that we endured, led me to four rules—which may never be of any particular value unless Newport establishes another fund, which I am now in the process of doing.

1. Never, ever put your brand on an entity you don't control.

2. Never, ever hire someone new to manage a really important endeavor. Better to hire a tried-and-trusted B-grade player, than an unknown (self-professed) star in the ascendant.
3. Never, ever, ever allow a limited partner (investor) to take equity in the general partner (fund manager).
4. Regardless of the goodies offered, never form a fifty-fifty joint venture with a party you don't know extremely well, through good times and bad.

Newport Capital gladly exited the funds management operations in April 2004. May God smile upon the long-suffering investors.

As the tech wreck bit, Newport Capital soldiered on with a reducing bank balance. Anticipating a three- or six-month dip in the market, I naively decided to maintain the infrastructure and pursue a counter cyclical strategy. This strategy became something of a bonfire of the vanities. Finally, in 2004, and after managing to expel the foreign body lodged in Newport Capital's vital organs (viz, the funds management operation), I went sane and downsized, retreating to a small office in North Sydney with Denis Quaintance, Chris Pearsall, Ben Cardillo, and Sasha—plus a particularly interesting gent introduced by Denis by the name of Vlad Dimitriou. Vlad is now working with IBA in Asia, a job befitting a gentleman and man-about-town of Vlad's stature.

Focused back on Newport Capital's core M&A and advisory business, with a small and excellent team, 2005, 2006, and 2007 have been kind years. The harder we work, the luckier we become. Apart from various surprises (a wise man named Neil Miller once explained to me that of every five surprises, four were bad surprises) Newport Capital is thriving, growing, and delivering a useful contribution.

A very wise man, Donald Grant McCreery who was one of the founders of Computer Resources Group, Fulbright Scholar, and graduate of the Wharton School, explained the magic circle of commerce to me in 1976: "Good people make good deals, good deals make good money, good money attracts good people, good people make good deals, etc.". This, to a degree, parallels my black hole theory. A substantial mass of intellect, passion, and energy (black hole) attracts like matter (high intellects and like-minded people) and this builds an enterprise.

We have become very selective in taking on new clients. Quality is as quality does. Our fee structures effectively bar waifs and strays from our list of clients, which pains me to the extent that I remain passionately committed to development of the indigenous ICT industry. We take on the occasional pro bono client, and the team berates me for doing so.

I have lost track of how many multi-millionaires Newport Capital has created—but of course we didn't really create any. They created themselves; we were just handmaidens at their exit performances. The tombstone file now occupies a lot of hard drive space.

This is definitely the best fun a human adult can have with their clothes on. I'll probably keep at it until either God takes me to Her warm breast; or at a Tuesday morning operations meeting, the team tells me it is in our mutual interest that I depart. I'll then finish the novel I started when I last retired after selling out of ATAC in 1985.

Chapter 1

Why Do Companies Make Acquisitions?

Most of the buy-side work Newport Capital has advised on over the past (nearly) twenty years is spawned by relatively common, but at times obscure, motivations.

- Deals come in over the transom, are thrown in the air, and those that land on the mantle piece are avidly pursued.
- Boards and executive teams get bored with the day-to-day grind, and decide to amuse themselves with M&A transactions. What you don't know much about is always enticing and easy, until you know about it.
- Business prospects are bleak, and so an acquisition strategy is invoked while there are still life signs in the dwindling share price.
- The coffers are overflowing, and rather than return capital to shareholders—who will only waste it—acquisitions are pursued.
- The chairman met a guy (or girl) in the chairman's (chairperson's) lounge at the airport, or at a Davos conference, and made a deal to acquire, needing only some finer detail to be added to what was crafted by genius in twenty minutes.
- A nasty competitor is causing stress in the market—often a whippersnapper new market entrant—and needs to be put into the acquisition shredder.

In rarer cases, a sophisticated board formulates an organic and inorganic growth plan, to leverage the balance sheet and the intellectual capital, by executing a carefully crafted acquisition strategy—with the board's, owners', or investors' backing—or backing of all of the foregoing.

IBM for example has a global quota for inorganic growth, region by region, country by country, business line by business line. Funding is allocated and bonuses depend on execution of the organic and inorganic targets. This catches everyone's attention. By a mix of organic and inorganic growth targets, the IBM omnibus moves strongly, eloquently, and sedately along, achieving year-on-year (YoY) growth—or heads roll. The end game is to achieve quarterly growth in earnings per share (EPS) to satisfy the market; the analysts; the CEO; the board; and, most importantly, the shareholders.

Not only this, but also firms, such as IBM, template (viz, define in some detail) the acquisition targets the line of business managers establish—some as back fill to expand existing business lines, but even more importantly acquisitions in market sectors targeted as growth engines for the future. Our sale of Classic Blue Group to IBM Australia was such a targeted acquisition.

So, when deal flow comes in over the transom, sophisticated buyers such as IBM have templates that can be used to determine strategic fit. It takes little time and effort to run a target against existing templates and decide whether or not to play. Opportunistic rushes of blood to the corporate head are rendered unlikely, and pleadings of advisors to buy a client on their books are ignored. Or even more poignantly, inbound deal flow is secondary to proactive efforts by M&A to survey the market and identify targets that match templates. Creativity and innovation are all in the initial strategy work, and not in target assessment on the run, as it should be. Measure three times, cut once!

A while back, I met with the CFO of a large Australian enterprise to discuss acquisition strategy. After some mumblings, it became apparent that the acquisition strategy was opportunistic and based largely on chance encounters and random thoughts of the line executives, plus inbound deal flow from trusted advisors—all seeking to get their trotters into the sizeable corporate trough.

Trying to create an analogy, I asked the CFO how the enterprise went about hiring new key executive staff. The answer was as expected—vacancies were determined by carefully crafted budgets and needs analysis, job specifications were prepared by human resources, trusted head hunters were briefed, searches were undertaken, best fits were determined, and short listed candidates were checked and interviewed. The best of the best were selected and appointed—with remuneration levels (in my terms, valuations) based on thorough industry remuneration surveys (in my terms, establishing comparables and running valuation models).

I rather gauchely compared the recruitment process to the established M&A process. "Is M&A less important than recruitment? Is it more okay to make poorly conceived acquisitions than to hire the wrong person for an important role?"

I wasn't exactly booted out the door, but my analogy was clearly not welcome. After a few minutes silence, the CFO acknowledged that the enterprise needed to take a more proactive approach to M&A. To my delight, the CFO told me he would engage Newport Capital to undertake a survey of a pesky sector where the board had determined that acquisitions would be made. Not only that, but Newport Capital would also assist in developing target templates.

Before the work was commissioned, alas the CFO resigned. Maybe he was targeted for acquisition and was best fit for a detailed target template?

So, in Newport Capital's view, acquisitions need to be approached strategically and methodically, as part of the business planning exercise. Inbound deal flow is worth having—if target templates exist. If proper target templates don't exist, then return to go and execute nothing until they do.

Digression #1 The Toothpaste Man

This particular client was nicknamed Toothpaste Man (TPM) by a very dear friend of mine, Kewan MacDonald, now deceased. Kewan was the founder of Mastersoft International, which survived Kewan's passing and is now run by an ex-client of mine, Gary Buttsworth. Kewan coined the name based on his view that the gentleman in question treated people like toothpaste—he squeezed the contents from the tube, and then discarded the tube. My assessment differs.

This engagement started when my mobile rang when I was between meetings in Melbourne. TPM as always cut to the chase—he needed to see me that day to engage me to sell his enterprise. TPM was in Sydney, but would meet me at a Melbourne hotel at 5.30 p.m., which he duly did.

I asked TPM to briefly describe the scope and scale of TPM's enterprise. TPM laid out a vision splendid and denoted the enterprise revenue as hovering around $60 million, with post—tax earnings of around $10 million. Furthermore, according to TPM, he was close to completing a transaction with a major brand IT vender, which I knew well, at a valuation of around $60 million. Later in the process, once I delved more deeply with the aid of TPM's CFO, it appeared that TPM had marginally overestimated (a rounding error?) the revenue and earnings—revenue was tracking at about $7 million and earnings before interest and tax (EBIT) was about negative $1 million. My first call to the MD of the major brand vender made it clear that he was no more than vaguely aware of TPM's enterprise, and based on my quick pitch had no interest whatsoever in learning more.

Further surprises were in store.

TPM had neglected to tell me that the enterprise was under the control of a well-known insolvency expert, as agent of the mortgagee in possession, appointed by TPM's bankers. Not only, but also, TPM insisted on dealing directly with a target that, according to TPM, was a long shot, and that for various reasons would not qualify for any fee payment to me if by some strange coincidence this target should transact. It had something to do with arrangements made by TPM with the bank's agent. No issue, TPM assured me—I had the rest of the market to play in!

Of course, a written offer arrived on the desk of the bank's agent in double quick time from the excluded target. The offer was a low ball, and the agent gave me thirty days to come up with another, superior offer. Something of a challenge, but off I went on the search for the premium buyer, at full pace.

By a mixture of good luck, hard work, and contacts, on day twenty eight, I met with the bank's agent and tabled a valid offer, subject to due diligence and overseas parent company approval, from a large buyer, which significantly trumped the offer from TPM's target.

Chapter 1: Why Do Companies Make Acquisitions?

All appeared to be progressing well, as the CFO and I worked through the due diligence process. The CFO, TPM, and I were called to a meeting by the bank's agent on short notice. The CEO and CFO of TPM's major (and most valuable) trading entity were already present when we arrived, both looking angry. The bank's agent then explained that the CEO and his CFO had submitted a management buy out (MBO) bid for that entity. Further more, the CEO and CFO had advised the bank's agent that if their bid was not immediately accepted, then they would walk out with the key staff and start up afresh—and take the key venders with them.

To his great credit, and as the MBO offer was far from the offer already in hand, the bank's agent asked the CEO if he owned a house—which in fact he did, and quite a nice one, too. The agent then explained that the penalty for aborting the due diligence and stealing the bank's assets, would be costly litigation that would immediately result in the bank being awarded damages for the full value of the extant offer, and the bank then proceeding to take the CEO's house and evict his wife and children without notice or patience. This effectively caused the immediate withdrawal of the MBO and the CEO and CFO went back to their work—with full enthusiasm restored.

The transaction completed, with the normal hiccups along the way. The funds were paid to the bank, and—as it happened—more than fully paid out the bank and left some change on the side for TPM. TPM was despondent—he explained to me that his original target's offer was at full value, as some consideration was to be paid directly to TPM into an offshore bank account. Hence the despondency.

On the afternoon of the completion meeting, the bank's agent and I drank a toast and TPM asked me to arrive at his new office—loaned by a friend—the next morning at 10.00 a.m., at which time we would agree to my fee and payment would be made.

I arrived to meet TPM and Mrs. TPM at the new office on time. TPM drew a cheque from his desk drawer and handed it to me. The amount of the cheque was exactly $50,000 more than my calculation of the fee due.

"Mate," TPM said, literally with tears forming, "I've added a bit to your fee, because you really did a great job, and saved my bacon and my house. You earned a little bonus."

I almost broke into sobs of gratitude and commiseration. How the mighty had fallen. TPM then wiped his eyes, rose up to his full height of not much, and said to Mrs. TPM, "Okay, darling, we are now at the end of the beginning, and the beginning of the end is behind us—let's go and make a sale."

So you can understand why I didn't agree with Kewan's assessment of TPM.

Chapter 2

An Acquirer's Tool Bag

Target Templates

The most basic tool in the bag is the acquirer's filter, a template or templates that describe in some detail the characteristics of targets that fit. The process of establishing templates derives from strategy sessions (strategic planning) where the most knowledgeable business managers, with or without consultants, determine key areas for corporate development.

There is a tendency for line management to focus on established business lines, which may or may not be the paths for acquisition focus. Back fill acquisitions, used to scale up existing operations with similar acquired businesses, have their place providing they don't represent sinking shareholders' funds into decaying products and services in mature, commoditized markets. The difficult part of strategic planning is to look over the horizon and pick relevant growth business opportunities. This is speculative and tricky, particularly in fast-moving sectors such as ICT. But, with careful research, analysis, and reflection, it can be done.

The target templates can be over-sophisticated and detailed to such a degree that nothing will pass through the filter. Alternatively, filters can be so loose that nearly everything qualifies and large particles can pass through the filter, in which case the filter itself is of little use.

Using the prepared templates, all targets identified can be scored and ranked against the template(s), whether they are incoming opportunities from random inbound deal flow or organizations identified from proactive outbound targeting work.

The output of template-based scoring of targets produces a short list, or highly ranked targets that can be pursued with confidence.

Sector Surveys

In manageable geographies such as Australia, it is feasible to survey an ICT sector in less than sixty days. This requires focused resources, but the results are well worth the cost and effort.

Newport Capital regularly undertakes ICT sector target surveys, ranks the identified targets against prepared templates, and prepares scored long and short lists. The client can then review the scored lists and select targets for engagement.

When Newport Capital undertakes surveys, we have the advantage of not having to disclose the client. We tend to obtain access to deeper data, including financial data, than a target would typically disclose to an industry player. Of course, the data we seek is always the data required to rank the target against a prepared template.

It is not possible to provide a guarantee that every target in a sector has been identified and profiled. However, we find that very few meaningful targets are missed in surveys. Surveys involve considerable desk-based research before contacts are made. Thankfully, the Internet and Google facilitate research. But so do trade publications, industry bodies (some of which publish member lists), the press, and other sources—including third-party research reports. Fortunately, over the past twenty years, Newport Capital has researched most ICT sectors, and popular sectors have probably been researched in the past two years from the initiation of a new survey. Previous research reports prove useful, but on every occasion we conduct a fresh review of the market sector and always find new and interesting targets. Some may have spun off from a larger parent through an MBO. Others may have been too small to appear on the radar of previous surveys, and have grown substantially. Another useful contraption is an established set of sector guides. Senior—and some quite junior—people operating in a sector will know a wide range of competitors and colleagues across their sector. Guides can provide useful assistance to identify targets of interest. In one recent survey, to our surprise (and it would have been to our embarrassment had we not contacted the guide) a guide identified a large and highly appetizing good fit target that we had not previously identified, and which became the number-one scored and ranked target.

The only downside of a properly rigorous sector survey is that the mystique of what's potentially out there tends to get frayed. Like the fisherman, some M&A people live in hope of a giant bass appearing in their M&A lake, when in fact none exists.

Comparables and Valuation Models

In the listed sector, comparables have some real meaning. Companies are conveniently grouped in sectors on the ASX, statistics are available for each sector and individual companies are compared to sector metrics. But even on the ASX, sector definitions and inclusions tend to be based on fuzzy data. It is quite feasible to examine and identify comparables on the Hong Kong GEM market, on the U.K. AIM market, on NASDAQ, and so on. But again, exact comparables are quite difficult to establish. Comparables tend to be used by bulge-bracket I-banks to provide comfort to buy-side clients, to the effect that a huge target valuation dropped out the end of a valuation model represents good value. Of course, the quantum of the success fee payable to the advisor is most frequently based on the value of the transaction, so the higher the valuation, the merrier the advisor. There are some good examples of huge valuations based on comparables in the Australian ICT market, none of which I will identify through fear of litigation.

Valuation models come in many shapes, sizes, and colours. All models basically try to calculate the present value of future free-cash flows, using a discount factor equal to the buyer's weighted average cost of capital (WACC).

The EPS accretion wand is another handy tool in the M&A conjuror's box of tricks. Ignoring the issues related to the projections on which EPS accretion prognostications are based, with or without synergies and leverage, EPS calculations produce interesting outcomes. Some prognostications announced to the market (e.g. Telstra's various acquisitions, including KAZ) project EPS accretion occurring at a future point (e.g. month 42.3759). Disregarding this actually means that the acquisition will be EPS excretive (viz, crapping shareholder value up against the boardroom wall) various levers can be pulled to determine EPS effects. For example, how will the acquisition be funded? If the transaction is funded by cash from a lazy balance sheet, and if the target is EBIT positive, then isn't the transaction immediately EPS accretive? The answer is maybe, depending on which levers in the valuation modeling process the buyer (or advisors) want to pull.

Apart from the WACC itself, there are many relatively subjective variables that enable valuation models to arrive at whatever answer you want. Here are just a few:

- Five-year profit and loss and resulting cash flow projections may be fine for a rust belt industrial with forty years trading history. In the ICT sector, one year can be a technology generation, subject to the nature of the industry sub-sector in question.
- Determining an end point value to crank into the DCF model is more mystery and imagination than science.
- Including estimated synergies—viz, savings or other leverage benefits manifesting in future projected profit and loss and cash flow—is challenging. Many buyers simply omit synergy effects, if they arise, so much the better. Other buyers with strong appetites leverage valuations by assuming huge synergies, savings, and leverage points. After all is said and done, most of this is lost in the wash and accountability is rare. Once the omelet is mixed, it is impossible to unscramble.
- Accurately determining the applicable WACC is again mysterious. One listed client claimed a WACC of 11 percent in an interest rate environment where overdraft rates were around 7 percent. If the total acquisition price could be borrowed from a bank at 8 percent it seemed difficult to understand a WACC of 11 percent. The client explained that the missing ingredient was the targeted

rate of return to shareholders, which formed part of the true WACC.

But leaving aside some of the challenges inherent in comparables and valuation modeling, there are some useful rules of thumb.

For example, cash payback period always attracts my attention. Again subject to the vagaries of profit and loss and cash flow projections, with or without a dash of synergies, plus a sprinkle of leverage benefits, it is not difficult to calculate after-tax cash payback on the funds invested—including any balance sheet top-up required to provide working capital for the acquired business.

If I spend $100, and earn after-tax cash of $20 (absolutely sustainable!), it seems that it will take me five years to get my money back. This is a good means of comparing available acquisitions. Waiting much longer, as is very often the case, to recover my cash investment seems like a long time. But then as average CEO tenures are probably less than five years maybe it doesn't really matter?

Another useful measure is simple return on investment (ROI) or rate of return. If I spend $100 on an acquisition and I make EBIT of $5 (you could argue net profit after tax [NPAT] to calculate actual cash on cash, but then I need to take the after-tax ROI on my funds at the bank in this case), it seems like I am making 5 percent per annum return on funds employed. Or, am I wrong? If I can make say 6 percent by placing my funds in a cash management account, then 5 percent invested in a risky transaction seems like a dud deal? I would expect a 15 percent or more return on funds employed, but then I may never execute a transaction.

Some buyers fixate on good will paid as part of a transaction. The accounting standards for good will have taken quite a leap forward (or backward depending on your perspective).

Good will—defined in my M&A handbook—is the difference between net tangible assets value (NTAV) of the balance sheet acquired (if there is one), and the total purchase price paid. In the old days, respectable companies wrote off good will at the acquisition date. More recently, good will could be amortized over the earning life of the asset. Today, the directors take a look at every balance date and determine the value of the good will.

This creates some very interesting scenarios. In challenging ICT sub-sectors such as products distribution, an owner can trade proudly for, say, ten years, earning EBIT all the way through, and retain earnings to provide working capital for the expanding business. Little do they realize that this may be financial folly. Coming to an exit transaction in year ten, the balance sheet NTAV has been built to, say, $90, and current year EBIT is, say, $25, and all of the NTAV is required to gear up the increasing turnover, and keep the bankers cool. An ROI analysis of funds employed to buy and operate the business, using a valuation of, say, 4 x EBIT = $100. Happy days you may think. Well actually, not so happy for the vender. Because all of the $90 NTAV is required to feed the business with working capital, and so the total amount of good will allowed is a measly $10.

Of course, if the business is debt funded, and the balance sheet NTAV remains positive, the scenario changes—or does it? Some more conservative buyers will point out that debt becomes their responsibility, and so must be included in total funds employed to calculate the internal rate of return (IRR). Outfoxed again!

Digression #2 Honest John (HJ)

I spent some years giving talks on M&A to pods of executives in The Executive Connection (TEC). I quite enjoyed this relief from the daily grind, and traveled to all capitals to deliver workshops. Most were well received, apart from one I conducted in Brisbane. An attendee chose to take me on regarding a matter of principle—I advanced the view that the purpose of an enterprise was to enrich its shareholders. The attendee took serious issue with my despicable view, arguing that the real ownership of any enterprise rests with the staff and executives. Today, after farces such as the Qantas debacle and the ministrations of the amigos at Telstra, I may be more amenable to the attendees view.

Chapter 2: An Acquirer's Tool Bag

One benefit from TEC seminars was word-of-mouth referrals. A referral arose from a TEC talk, and I was approached by Honest John to sell his enterprise—a call centre operation. Warning bells rang when HJ spent twenty minutes in our first meeting explaining the depth of his honesty and ethics.

HJ proceeded to outline the marvels of his enterprise. He went on to say that at a direct marketing conference he had attended recently in the United States, he had been approached by a large call centre operator regarding the possible acquisition of his enterprise. There was no traction as yet in these discussions, but HJ wanted me to tease out this opportunity, as well as round up some more buyers. The enterprise was tracking at about $6 million revenue and was doing marginally better than breaking even. HJ explained that he was targeting a valuation of about $5 million, which, based on the financial tracking I explained, was optimistic. My drive-by, wet-finger valuation was around $2.5 million.

Over the course of several meetings, HJ explained that he agreed that my valuation estimate was probably reasonable, given that Newport had transacted several call centre sales, and Newport knew call centre sector valuations quite well. HJ suggested, in response to my fee proposal, that we agree in principle that my proposal would stand when and if a transaction began to emerge. Out of fairness to Newport, HJ would pay daily rates plus expenses up to that point. Of course, I documented this arrangement in correspondence and proceeded—with a colleague, Alf Stamp (now CFO of Les Fallick's highly prosperous Principle Advisory)—to execute the transaction process.

Early research of the U.S.-based buyer company that had approached HJ at the U.S. conference revealed an interesting event. The U.S. company had announced a major deal with a global credit card issuer, requiring twenty-four/seven call centre services—the sun never sets, etc. Of particular interest, was a commitment to establish a call centre in the country of Australia! Eureka! And moreover, the Australian call centre was to be fully operational in a very short time. Double Eureka!

Alf and I worked hard and fast to prepare a suitably enticing IM, which when provided to the potentially interested U.S.-based party would make it clear that advisors were engaged, and any transaction would be contested.

I made contact with the vice chairman of the U.S. company (code-named Honk), who was the gent who had approached our client at the U.S. conference. I agreed to send Honk the IM by fast courier and was called soon after dispatching the IM by Honk to say he would arrive in Sydney several days later. I arranged to collect Honk from his flight.

Various meetings were held with Honk and HJ. In one of the more advanced meetings, Honk asked me to indicate an acceptable value for HJ's enterprise, to which I gave the normal I-banker response that the market sets the value, not the vender etc.

HJ was by this stage becoming quite frenzied. This seemed like a good time to remind HJ of our arrangement regarding fees, as confirmed by me in correspondence. HJ looked shocked, and said this was not a time to raise this issue, as no deal was on the table. "Oh, oh, what's happened to HJ?" I thought at the time. But Alf assured me that HJ would behave properly etc, and Alf was a good assessor of humans—having been a star soccer player and coach.

So, soon thereafter, HJ, Honk, Alf, and I met at HJ's premises, and we gazed into Honk's baby blues.

"What would you like to say Honk?" I asked.

"Well," said Honk, "my due diligence confirms that HJ's enterprise is the right operation for us to buy. I don't want to have a lengthy debate, as there are various timing drivers that I need to keep in mind" (we know Honk, I thought). "So my offer is . . . $20 million."

I flicked my attention to HJ, who was rapidly turning purple, which was convenient as this could be interpreted by Honk as a sign of displeasure. Not to be deterred, I replied, "We are pleased to consider your offer, but I must advise you that HJ has instructed us to pursue a price of $25 million."

Honk, who was not short of a few measly millions, thought for a while and retorted, "Let's split the difference and do $22.5 million."

Chapter 2: An Acquirer's Tool Bag

HJ now started foaming at the mouth, as HJ was wont to do at times of stress. I turned to HJ and said, "HJ, I know this is short of your target, but I feel that I can, based on the status of other bidders, encourage you to deal at Honk's offer price."

In a tiny voice HJ replied, "Oh, ok, I accept."

The next piece lives in my memory as if it were yesterday. Honk then said to HJ, "Well, HJ, how would you like to be paid? We can issue you shares in the U.S. entity at a small discount from market, we can pay you cash on completion, or a mixture of cash and shares."

HJ looked puzzled and turned to me and asked, "What do you think?"

I responded, "Well, HJ, this is entirely up to your judgment, but I would seriously consider cash." (My logic was that if Honk was tooling around the world making offers at this level of valuation, then the U.S. listed scrip might take a hiding).

HJ turned to Honk, and launched into his honest man dissertation, then added, as an honest man, "Honk, I must say that I deeply admire you and the fine enterprise that you and your colleagues have built. I will be deeply honoured to be a part of your company. If we can agree that I will remain the CEO of the Australian subsidiary, I would be very happy and comfortable to take the price all in shares." Honk smiled. HJ was obviously intoxicated by his own exhaust fumes.

Honk left the building. HJ, Alf, and I felt like swinging from the chandelier. To strike while the iron was still white hot, I said to HJ, "Well, HJ, it now seems that we have a done deal. Honk has put his Sydney lawyers in touch with your lawyers to draft the contracts, and I expect that the deal will complete. Honk is in a hurry, so let's make sure we are all on the same page regarding our fee, as we have previously discussed.

I can't recall HJ's exact words, but he burst into a tirade. "How dare you raise this yet again. You know as well as I do that we agreed that you would be paid daily rates for your services, and that's what is going to happen. If you have any issues, then take them up with David (HJ's lawyer) and David will no doubt disabuse you of any misconceptions you may have on fees. You can leave now, your work is done."

Alf and I felt it was better to regroup rather than take on HJ at this emotional point in HJ's life, so we exited.

Not long after this last meeting with HJ, we received by courier HJ's cheque for the time we had billed up to the last meeting, and not only the cheque, but also two HJ company tee shirts that HJ handed out to staff and customers at Christmas.

I suspect that Alf used his tee shirt for an inappropriate purpose—my remains in my cabinet of souvenirs—filed under "c."

We pursued HJ and his lawyer through various twists and turns. But HJ was resolute—we had been paid in full for our services, and any further discussions would not be tolerated. We considered legal action, but HJ's lawyer had made his views clear—a letter from Newport to HJ purporting to document a verbal agreement was of little value at law. HJ would deny any such agreement had been reached, and basically we could get lost.

We continued to deal cordially with Honk, and subsequently raised some capital from Honk's enterprise for another client, which was something of a windfall. I got to know Honk well, and in one discussion asked Honk where he lived. Honk lived in Brussels, but spent the summers at his beach house at Cap D'Antibes. I remember saying that I always found moving to the beach tiresome, packing up, then the drive with a car full of kids, animals, and belongings was tiresome.

Honk explained that this was not really a burden to Honk or Mrs. Honk, as all that was required was notice to the cook, housekeeper, chauffer, gardener, and pilot (who drove Honk's small jet parked at a nearby airfield), and his household was quickly and painlessly conveyed to his beach house. Trying to gracefully remove my foot from my mouth, I asked Honk where at Cap D'Antibes his beach house was located, as I had visited there a few years previously. Honk explained that his summer house was, in fact, located smack bang on the Cap, and occupied a Cap frontage of about 1.5 kilometers, which was convenient as Honk and Mrs. Honk preferred privacy.

Chapter 2: An Acquirer's Tool Bag

I always received very nice original-art Christmas cards from Honk until his death some years ago.

HJ was, after some months, sent on gardening leave from his new enterprise. The share price of the U.S. entity plunged to about 20 percent of the price of the issue to HJ—the market dispenses its own form of justice.

Chapter 3

Why Do Most Acquisitions Fail?

Various statistics published by knowledgeable firms show very high failure rates for acquisitions. A rate of 85 percent-plus is not an unusual figure.

The real issue is that acquisitions have many moving parts, and managing all of the moving parts is beyond the ability of most acquirers. Just a few of the major moving parts are as follows.

Culture

I define culture as values. Companies don't have values—apart from value statements put on Web sites and notice boards—people have values. And the higher the rank of the person in an enterprise, the more important their values become. Some very senior people I have encountered in business are the types of people you would like to invite to your beach house for a long weekend. To others you would not offer accommodation in your dog's kennel.

Like schools, companies take their cultural lead from the boss. Good boss, good values, good staff equals good school. Nasty, political, conniving, self-focused, self-aggrandizing, lazy, spendthrift (on the expense account!), otherwise mean boss equals same values spreading through the organization, top to bottom, with good people heading for the exits. Given that most human beings live their values (and those that don't aren't worth having onboard), and given that most successful companies succeed on the basis of their unfair quotient of human capital—defined as smarter and more knowledgeable people trying their hardest—there are some basic rules that need to be observed.

- Other than where an acquirer consciously is seeking to remediate a toxic culture, disparate cultures shouldn't be mixed and shouldn't be acquired. Acquiring a bunch of conniving vagabonds

into a proper-values company culture will bring tears before bedtime.
- Toxic cultures are best remediated before acquisitions are attempted. Launching major cultural change by acquisition probably will see the acquired human capital depart for friendlier, more compatible environments.
- Use an expert in human resources (not just in operational health and safety) to assess a target's culture. There are firms that specialize in the black arts, to good effect, as a means of risk reduction.
- Provide careful post-transaction care and maintenance of the acquired human capital. Make them feel at home. Have the acquirer's boss talk to them all—openly and frankly, as the truth is a powerful driver.

Cultural mismatches are probably a major cause of acquisition failures. Most, if not all, companies are built on relationships—internal and external. When the human capital is lost, the relationships are lost, and a juicy, high-potential acquisition can quickly turn into a handful of dust.

Integration

Integration planning is a chestnut of note.

Really poorly managed and inexperienced acquirers, sometimes focused on evening scores with a competitor they have acquired (to get even), frequently tell lies to the acquired people. "No jobs will be lost. There will be no change in roles for the foreseeable future. Remuneration packages will be reviewed and brought up to scratch with the acquirer's higher pay rates. There will be new company cars for all and reduced sales quotas for all reps. Not to mention, annual bonuses that will bring tears of joy to your bank manager's eyes."

While the real intent is to pounce on the poor acquirees, be as nasty as possible to get the head count down to lift earnings, change the organization structure on day one, and make the acquired CEO a special projects manager reporting to the tea lady.

Clever integration is possible. It's an intricate task and sometimes heads must be made redundant. The manual says to plan redundancies carefully, complete them swiftly, and complete the entire integration in the first quarter following the transaction. Tell everyone the truth about integration plans early in the post-acquisition honeymoon period, and be truly sad with and about the dearly departed. Again, the services of a human resources expert help considerably to de-risk integration plans and execute the integration itself. A capable human resources person provides a convenient shoulder to cry on, and is someone to receive expressions of fear and other feelings.

One of the hugely successful ICT sector listed companies—UXC—has a crafty strategy for integration: Do nothing. They figure if it's good enough to buy, don't try to fix it. Apart from some back office integration, UXC is about backing and empowering teams to do more than they otherwise could achieve. UXC helps acquired companies to acquire; makes them feel important; cements the key people into the organization with well-structured, highly motivating, simple earn outs; and rewards the achievers without trying to dud them by tampering with the earn outs. So UXC, like many successful acquirers, is really a holding company for a conglomeration of profit-producing businesses. Who really cares if this is blessed by McKinsey & Co.? It works just fine.

Change

Rule 1: Anything a chief executive/board knows little about is easy to enhance and improve.
> So, a typical scenario post acquisition is that inspired leaders initiate changes—to improve the yield post transaction.

Rule 2: Anything that you really start to understand is complex and difficult to materially change for the better, unless it was and still is run by a bunch of no hopers, in which case you are really in for it!

Experienced acquirers take time to move the tectonic plates on which an acquired business is founded. Pre-transaction integration planning at a relatively cursory level apart (fire six accountants, four receptionists and three tea ladies—and be careful to have your human resources advisor check for likely impacts—the tea ladies may be the opinion leaders, etc.), most seasoned acquirers wait and learn before moving the tectonic plates. A formal, ongoing learning and review process is mandatory, with the panel including key acquiring and acquired people, is mandatory.

Most people resist change, as it brings with it stress and the need to learn new routines. The impact of change can be mediated by education. Too few acquirers spend the appropriate time and money to educate acquiring and acquired people to cope with necessary change.

Attitude

Skilled and experienced human resources people can establish, monitor, and measure care and maintenance programs to maximize value added by acquired human capital. One such professional I worked with took the role of the adopting parent, cherishing the adopted children and applying discipline as reasonably required.

This particular executive, a lady of generous attitudes, considerable discipline, and quality values, made it her mission to create positive karma and attitude in the acquirer's executive team. She counseled and appraised the acquirees, but spent even more time and effort counseling the acquirer's executive team. The dividends were huge.

One acquiring CEO booted the acquired CEO out of his corner office, which boasted a harbour view, and installed himself therein on Day 1. The intent apparently was to show who now is the boss in a clear and visible way. The effect on the acquired CEO and his troops was less than positive. The acquired CEO, having a sense of humour and a bonus paid by his erstwhile employer for helping to get the transaction over the line, went and bought a Porsche, and parked it in the most conspicuous possible parking bay—"up you for your lunch" was the signal, and the troops responded with negative attitudes for months, and months.

Attitude, like culture, comes from the top.

PTM Reflux

PTM (Paid Too Much) Reflux is quite deadly and threatens the life of the acquired business.

When appetite to acquire is ravenous, egos reign free, the valuation model is cranked up using all possible leverage (unrealistic post-acquisition, high-growth projections, large helpings of synergy savings, and oodles of leverage from cross selling, etc.), and the outcome is inevitable. The executives that sponsored the valuation modeling (who, of course, will blame the advisors who have banked their inflated fee and retired to the Costa Smerelda) may actually have the eyes of the board trained on them to deliver the projections.

It can quickly become apparent that the projections and valuation modeling were wildly optimistic, and will never be delivered, causing angst and PTM reflux in the executive team.

Rather than 'fessing up to a gross error in judgment, the guilty party will usually weigh into the hapless acquired executive team with machetes honed and start cutting the entrails out of the acquired business. This works for a short period, and the monthly management accounts initially show vigilance and profit-and-loss improvement. However, this halo effect is not sustainable, and the acquired business starts a death spiral. It all makes spread sheet sense—fire most of the sales team (indolent, overpaid prima donnas), hack into the ongoing research and development effort, increase prices across the board, apply the screws to all venders, etc. Most of the intellectual capital departs, customers terminate, and venders seek other customers who will pay fair market prices for their goods and services. And, of course, competitors smell blood and predate.

Intentional Fraud

Fraudulent intent, though relatively rare, can destroy acquisitions very rapidly and cause massive value hemorrhages.

Fraudulent intent can exist with either the buyer or the seller.

A nasty buyer can set up a transaction for post-transaction feasting. Typical tricks include light due diligence followed my massive reps and warranty claims. If the vender or venders happen to be involved in running the acquired business, this tends to produce negative sentiments. Re-jigging post-transaction financials to deplete earn outs is another favourite. Again, if the venders happen to be recipients working in the acquired business, morale quickly dives and more energy is spent on litigation and arguments than is spent on delivering results.

Fraudulent venders can use a variety of ploys to trick buyers. Apart from bare-face lies regarding past trading results, balance sheets, sales funnel prospects, dark morale, departing venders that have served notice, etc.; there can be subtleties that wreck the acquired business and even the business of the acquirer.

Most buyers are relatively poorly equipped to guard against vender fraud. People tend to rely on what they want to hear, and are not expecting nor accustomed to fraudulent behaviour. Light pre-transaction due diligence can miss some obvious exposures, and reliance on vender reps and warranties is a poor substitute for adequate and risk-mitigating due diligence.

Getting it Wrong

Even the most expertly planned and executed perfect fit transactions can go awry. Common causes for failure include:
- poor strategy—measure once and then try to repeatedly cut;
- lack of leverage and synergies;
- lack of growth potential in the acquired business;
- lack of domain expertise and knowledge;
- rushed or excessively delayed integration; alien cultures;
- lack of buy-in and commitment from the CEO and board;
- lack of stickiness of key executives, viz no deferred or contingent consideration.

Getting it wrong, really wrong, is aggravated by denial, which is the normal reaction to pear-shaped transactions. The only effective action in dealing with a materially flawed transaction is to recognize failure and reduce exposure. Downscaling an acquired business and forcing profitability is tough, but mostly achievable. Then when life signs have been confirmed, fully integrate the acquisition and take the write-downs. This is easy to say perhaps, but in my experience very difficult to fess up to. It is nevertheless, the only viable course of action.

Digression #3 Adventures in Paradise?

I consider the CEO of this interesting client company a mate—we still talk to each other.

The company—code-named Bytes—was backdoor listed into a shell/cash box, with consideration paid entirely in scrip in the listed entity. The listed entity had been controlled by a team of sharp, well-connected chaps who knew their way around the market.

My mate tells me that on completion of the transaction, with my mate then installed as CEO of the listed entity, he returned to his office and set about calculating the various ownership percentages in the listed entity—really, this is what he did. "Eureka," he exclaimed, my mates and I are now the controlling shareholders of the listed entity, and not the sharp, well-connected chaps in town.

First thing the following day, my mate called the chairman (one of the smart, well-connected chaps in town code-named the Manchurian) and advised he would be calling by the chairman's office to collect several handy items—the corporate seals, the cheque book, and a bankers advice signed by the chairman establishing my mate and his second in command as the bank signatories—or else an EGM (Extraordinary General Meeting) would ensue!

Being well informed; the smart, well-connected chaps cried uncle, and my mate and his team took full operational and financial control of the listed entity.

Chapter 3: Why Do Most Acquisitions Fail?

Some months later, my mate shooed the smart, well-connected lot off the board, installed a friendly as chairman and took off to conquer the world. The enterprise took on the impedimenta befitting an emerging global giant. Such was the stature of the enterprise, that Newport was then engaged to make a placement of some millions.

The investor—a terribly nice chap from Europe who played jazz piano—took a shine to the U.S.-based sales manager and relegated my mate, who was still on the board in a watered-down state, to a desk in the staff canteen.

Under the tutelage of the European-based investor/jazz pianist, the newly installed U.S.-based president adopted a gutsy business plan to lead with expense, thinking revenue would surely follow. It didn't. Shock and horror ensued. After a couple of nasty quarterly reports, the entity was suspended from trading by the ASX.

Enter my mate, who brought in the cavalry, which included Newport and me.

My mate and I then set out to trim the corporate sails. We fired the U.S. president and substantially downsized and restructured operations. Basically, if someone was a consumer of the corporate bread and butter versus a generator of said bread and butter, they were allowed to pursue other opportunities.

Remarkably, the purgatives administered worked well and worked quickly. The suspended entity was relisted on the ASX, my mate was carried triumphantly on the shoulders of the shareholders at the next AGM, Newport cashed in its sizeable chunk of options, and peace was restored in the land. My mate then progressively sold down his equity and is now peacefully employed writing a doctorial dissertation and enjoying academic life to the fullest.

Unfortunately, my mate—true to his own description—was great at start-ups and fix ups, and truly capable of becoming bored and then moving on. He sold his shares and did quite well! After he left, the entity failed, and not a trace remains.

The truly poignant element of this story is that it is wise to do the numbers and work out who is in control of a listed entity—before and after a scrip-based acquisition.

Chapter 4

Why Are Companies Sold?

For the purpose of this section, I will disregard the major part of the exit market, where listed companies' boards sell their enterprises. Premiums to share price are the main drivers. Recent examples, such as Coles and Qantas have their particular spins—and outcomes. Raiders like breaking up lazy balance sheets and crystallizing underlying values. But these transactions, while they command the headlines in the financial press, are beyond my experience, and my particular interest.

In the privately held sector, and with an ICT and related bias, there are many splendid reasons for sales and/or exits.

Exceptional and completely unexpected valuations are certainly a hot topic. Recent examples include the purchase of Mincom by Francisco Partners, and the purchase of KAZ by Telstra—the later being a significantly value excretive transaction for Telstra. The purchase of Trading Post by Telstra's subsidiary Sensis was similarly harshly value excretive.

Mere mortals observe these transactions that go completely off the valuation spreadsheet and wonder what the post-transaction future will hold. Private equity players have their own particular views of the world; partly driven, I suspect, by front-end fees payable to themselves, by themselves or related entities, or managed OPM; and partly by a sense of one-upmanship.

Most sellers I have encountered fall into the categories outlined below.

Distressed Sellers

The distressed seller is usually at the end of his tether, and grave prospects motivate a transaction. Desperate sellers typically want speed of execution rather than premium valuations. Most buyers can recognize this category of seller and avoid them when possible. Decaying financials, departing key staff (always look at the payroll records for the past twelve months to measure churn), anguished customers, and predation by competitors denote a rotting carcass.

I avoid desperate sellers—marketing a rotting carcass is very difficult; but, more importantly, denigrates Newport Capital's brand value. If an advisory firm sells only high-quality merchandise, their offerings are welcome. If they purvey dead meat, no one wants to bother looking.

However, not all distressed sellers need to be avoided. Some years back, I was engaged by a notable ICT sector entrepreneur who needed to sell a valuable operating business due to distress arising from another group entity on which he had bet the farm.

His bankers had appointed an agent of the mortgagee in possession, and he was pressed to sell the viable operating entity. I was pleased to execute a sale to a large multinational buyer. My client was pleased with the outcome, which more than paid out the bank and left some surplus cash for the client. The next step was to sell the entity on which the farm had been bet. To my surprise, another large multinational picked up the pieces for a significant value. My client was even more pleased as it vindicated his investment decision.

Life Cycle Venders

As baby boomers reach their use-by dates, they will seek exits if there is no intention to pass the business to the family and build a dynasty. Wise owners have attended to succession planning by developing a management structure that will survive, and perhaps even prosper, after their exit.

As identified in reports and surveys published by various large accounting firms, there are literally thousands of exits banking up for near-term execution. Many will be in retail and small mum-and-pop businesses, which may not be transactable.

Spin-Offs and Strategic Sales

Increasingly, large corporates are focusing on strategy and divesting no-longer-core activities. IBM Australia sold its Wangaratta plant to a financial buyer. Fujitsu and a financial investor sold the data centre entity acquired from the NSW Government. Capgemini sold its New Zealand operations to the management in an MBO, which was subsequently sold to H-P for a tidy profit. Atos Origin sold its Australian subsidiary to Fujitsu—I managed the sale. CSC sold its health informatics business to Neil Cullimore and mates, who on-sold to iSoft, now acquired by Gary Cohen's IBA Health, for a large multiple of everything.

These types of transactions can be described as strategic sales, where an asset is no longer categorized as "core." In August 2007, Hansen Corporation sold its managed services operations (managed by Newport Capital) to a trade buyer, in order to focus on and fund acquisitions close to Hansen's core utilities billing systems activity. Destra sold its communications business for a handsome valuation to a listing entity seeking to bulk up. Newport Capital's client, Cellnet, spun out its Mercury Mobility mobile content operation—not in a sale, but in a listing transaction.

It is refreshing that large corporations transact strategic sales and spin-outs. These transactions illustrate two key principles. First, that strategy is fundamental to inorganic transactions—both sales and acquisitions. Without the benefit of documented strategy, all inorganic transactions become opportunistic and random. Second, these types of transactions illustrate the importance of leadership as an essential ingredient.

In the case of IBM or Atos Origin, the decisions to divest were taken at the highest level and firmly prosecuted through to completion. Valuation was secondary to completion, but of course money is always important and welcome. But these types of transactions are not distressed seller transactions, so speed of execution and valuation are secondary issues. The nature of the buyer can be very important—strategic venders prefer not to sell to competitors for obvious reasons. They prefer financial buyers, or local Australian entities without offshore, potentially competitive, activities.

Because divestments and spin-offs are not primarily motivated by valuation, these types of opportunities are favoured by buyers. Various buyers have generated substantial fortunes from purchases of non-core businesses from major corporates, including multinationals. Selling such non-core activities is a relatively new phenomenon. Going back ten or fifteen years, non-core activities were just closed down, a type of razed earth policy. Today, particularly in the technology markets as they become increasingly commoditized, even a few million dollars can't be discarded.

Habitual Sellers/Serial Entrepreneurs

Many sell-side clients of Newport Capital—Classic Blue Group sold to IBM Australia is a good example—want to crystallize the value they have created in their business over many years, with a clear view of an exit. Most are prepared to hang around post transaction for an orderly hand over. But a wise buyer (e.g., IBM) knows that a seller's motivation to continue to make extraordinary efforts to grow and improve an enterprise post sale is inversely related to their bank balance.

When a habitual seller engages an advisor, such as Newport Capital, the clear message to prospective buyers is maximization of sale proceeds. The advisor will use various tools to communicate this message to targets. Tools include a clearly defined schedule and process, creation of competitive tension, and other less obvious tools such as circulation of frequently asked questions (FAQ) documents. FAQ documents make it apparent that multiple parties are asking different questions, and the documents create a level playing field for all prospective purchasers.

Some sellers have consciously built their enterprise for an eventual payday. Others have simply built their business because it was there. But, when most SMB owners reach a point where they really believe their share certificates can be converted to cash at bank, they cry, "Show me the money."

Some people, including line managers in large vender organizations, will moralize endlessly about such displays of self-interest and plain old greed. Such people tend not to have invested the very hard yards required

Chapter 4: Why Are Companies Sold?

to build a valuable and viable business, and their sentiments are not much more than sour grapes.

Some sellers in this category go on serially—creating new enterprises, which succeed or fail. Richard Graham, Chairman of ASX-listed Infomedia is a prime example of a serial entrepreneur. I acted for Richard and his partners, including David Fox—hugely rich from the sale of an astrology Web site business that David and his wife created from his sale proceeds—and the Herzberg family, in selling InfoMagic, a software distribution business, to Unisys.

In the backroom of Infomagic, and fully disclosed to Unisys—was a technology in research and development called Microcat. Microcat was the next step in the development path of spare parts systems beyond microfiche-based systems.

Bob Tway, the Unisys managing director, was less than enthused with Microcat, even though Unisys was involved in the motor vehicle sector—mainly in the United States.

I recall the meeting with Bob Tway and Richard Graham, when Bob questioned Richard on the Microcat technology—still in research and development. While Unisys had focus on the automotive sector in the United States, Bob was no domain expert. Richard gave Bob an unvarnished view of Microcat. After a few minutes of consideration Bob excluded Microcat from the Infomagic purchase—I know not why. It's interesting that the highly successful Infomedia Ltd. arose from the Microcat technology developed within Infomagic, based on an entirely serendipitous decision by Bob Tway to leave the IP with the Infomagic venders.

Richard—with Myer Herzberg in tow—went on to further develop Microcat into the core of what is now ASX-listed Infomedia. Richard converted Unisys' reject into many millions of dollars in a relatively short period. Infomedia, which was holding its AGM at Narrabeen Surf Club and providing fish and chips wrapped in the Sydney Morning Herald (or maybe it was the Financial Review) to the shareholders and analysts for lunch, much to their delight, now runs revenues approaching $100 million and makes an EBIT (in good years) of about 30 percent on revenues—stunning!

Digression #4 Luck of the Irish

Through some connections involving a client and Jay Hennock—who subsequently joined Newport and added considerable luster to the firm's corporate cluster—Newport was engaged to raise capital for an unlisted client who happened to be the recipient of considerable funding from one of Australia's highest net worth family investment vehicles.

This Australian-based company (code-named LOTIR) was involved in highly innovative Internet gaming technology, at a relatively early stage of the gaming technology life cycle. There was something of a fracas emerging in the United States, where the Bible belt was encouraging the U.S.-regulator to ban Internet gaming as a tool of the devil. But actual bans were to emerge later.

Knowing most of the active Australian venture capitalists—of which there were at the time probably no more than twelve or so really active—the obvious game plan was to present LOTIR to the local venture capital community. After several months of full-on efforts, working closely with the CEO, who was of Irish origin like many Australians particularly in the colony's early days of British migration from prison hulks on the Thames, and board, prospects appeared bleak. As is typically the case in venture capitalist focused capital raisings—both then and now—normal venture capital fundamentals applied:
- Every investment must have the potential to be a ten bagger (viz 1,000 percent return)—and quickly.
- The exit must be clearly defined.
- The technology must be disruptive and applicable to global markets.
- The executive team must demonstrate capacity to leap tall buildings, stop speeding locomotives, and catch bullets—preferably in their teeth.

Chapter 4: Why Are Companies Sold?

- The key risks must be controllable or preferably non-existent—no technical, managerial, financial, operational, or other nasty risks evident.
- The investee must be able to demonstrate capital adequacy to the exit point from the moment of the investment.
- There must be an irresistible value proposition.
- Etc.

The closest we got to funding was when Macquarie—in the days of Sandy Lockhart and Mike Traill—expressed interest but at a disappointingly low valuation. Aristocrat almost pounced, but deflected.

"What to do, what to do," said the board. With cash evaporating and insolvency maybe ninety days down the track, what options existed?

As it happened, my sector research had involved a close look at various U.S. gaming sector companies. Armed with a map of the United States, I plotted the course of a road show to pitch to U.S.-based strategic investors who might be interested in jumping on the not-yet-banned Internet gaming market.

So, after a week of phone calls to the U.S. enterprises, the CEO—whom I shall call Lucky—and I set out on a ten-day road show, equipped with some nice slides and some crumby hotels booked nearby the corporate lairs of the U.S.-based targets. Pitch we did—and Lucky pitched admirably. Tiring, and on the final stages of our whirlwind tour of the United States, we came to Reno, Nevada—the home of a very large player in the gaming systems business (code-named Megacorp).

The board was assembled in the conference room as Lucky and I entered with some trepidation. The chairman, a particularly gentlemanly and pleasant elder statesman, welcomed us and noted that he would depart in thirty minutes by helicopter to attend a grand new casino opening. Lucky hit them with everything he had. Forty minutes into the meeting, the chairman called his personal assistant and deferred the helicopter ride.

After another hour, the deal was basically made—Megacorp would invest $15 million for a 30 percent share in LOTIR, a due diligence team would be dispatched at the earliest possible date, and completion of the transaction would quickly follow.

The chairman and I happened to pee in adjoining urinals at a break in proceedings. "Tell me," he said, "you're from Australia, do you know a guy named Mr. X? We met with Mr. X before you and Lucky arrived and, boy, were we impressed. We intend to hire Mr. X as our Asia Pacific CEO."

Well, I did happen to know Mr. X—quite well indeed. Mr. X had a reputation for supreme arrogance and a pension for tanking enterprises and then moving on. So what do I tell the chairman? The wise course would have been to deny any knowledge. But I am not always up for the low-risk option.

Both "put away," I turned to the chairman and said, "bad call," with emphasis on the bad.

It was a poetic moment, there at the urinals. The chairman said only "Uh ha," which was adequate.

Nothing more was said. Mr. X and I coincidentally met at the baggage roundabout at Sydney terminal, his Gucci bags with first class tags attached, preceding mine by a substantial margin. "What have you been up to?" Mr. X inquired. "Oh, I've been doing some human resources consulting for a U.S. firm," I replied and left it at that. Mr. X was not appointed to the Megacorp role. I wonder if he ever found out why.

Lucky and I then proceeded to Los Angeles, where Lucky and I spent a luxurious thirty-six hours recovering from our travails, with Lucky regularly weeping on my sleeve about how he had been done dirty by his HNW investor family, and the world in general. I must say I liked Lucky—my mother was of Irish descent.

Back home, all was joyous. The Megacorp team arrived in short order, completed the due diligence, briefed the lawyers to prepare the contracts, and left. At one point in the due diligence preparation, I asked my colleague—Lindsay Boyle, a very smart Irish lady with steel in her demeanor—to read the board minutes that had been requested by Megacoprp. Lindsay—now working in a senior role at the Bank of Ireland I have been told—spotted a set of recent board minutes stating, "Make sure the hook is fully embedded in Megacorp before the final arm wrestle on pricing, etc." Lindsay judiciously blacked out the offending wording. This is a salient lesson regarding preparation and sanitization of due diligence materials.

The LOTIR chairman, appointed by the HNW family investor, effectively hijacked the Megacorp transaction, and I was left to observe from a distance, but with strong continuing interest generated by the fee in store. Losing control of a transaction in train with a material risk-based fee is dyspeptic. The transaction/success fee was based on what I originally thought to be an irksome matrix structure invented by the chairman—where the fee increased as a function of the pre-money value and the quantum of the investment.

Post the completion euphoria, and to my considerable chagrin, Lucky decided to stiff Newport on the fees and went incommunicado—my attempts to solve the matter with the HNW family and the chairman were to no avail. I finally managed to largely collect, but under sad circumstances, which soured the victory.

As a postscript, hanging off LOTIR was another unrelated Internet start-up, held out from the transaction with Megacorp. This quirky Internet business was subsequently sold for nearly $40 million to a major media group and Lucky really lucked in. LOTIR faded from view once the U.S. regulators became feisty and banned Internet gaming—with other jurisdictions following the U.S. lead.

Chapter 5

Buy-Side Transactions

The following commentary on buy-side M&A work is biased toward an advisor's view of the world. However, I expect that most of the text will be relevant to an in-house M&A practitioner's view. I have worked both as an M&A advisor, and as an in-house practitioner. I think the key differences are that an in-house practitioner executes fewer transactions, makes less money on the upside, but is paid and gets to eat regularly. There is also a mystical bond of trust between in-house practitioners and their clients. Independent advisors tend to be treated with less trust and are assumed to have various secret agendas.

Methodology

I am proud that Newport Capital has evolved a buy-side methodology, which has been honed over nearly twenty years of advising buy-side clients. At first blush, the methodology appears too elaborate to many clients. There are steps in the methodology, and particularly some pre-engagement steps (pre-engagement due diligence) that appear excessively particular and picky.

Practitioners early in their careers expect that hooning around their business sector armed with the corporate cheque book is as close to paradise as one can get on this mortal coil. As with a rule enunciated previously, things you know little about are simple, appealing, and satisfying. Things you know a lot about tend to be complex, demanding, and frustrating.

Armed with a logical and effective methodology, reasonable intellect, good industry sector knowledge and reputation, wide-established sector relationships, strong negotiating skills, a pension for sales, and strong financial skills and understandings, M&A buy-side work is easy. Anyone can do it.

Of course, approaching targets from the executive floor of an industry player and seeking deep disclosure of confidential business information from actual or quasi-competitors has its challenges. A third-party advisor's analysts and practitioners tend to gather more useful information through a survey effort.

Buy-Side Collateral

It is completely normal and expected that an IM will be provided to targets in a sell-side engagement process. I believe that it is equally, or even more important to provide buy-side targets with a profile of the acquirer, to sell the buyer to the seller. The more alluring the target, the more important this becomes.

This is particularly relevant in a full-proactive buy-side engagement that is expected to transact multiple acquisitions over an extended project period.

Apart from the buyer client's standard glossies, a succinct buyer IM can include really useful information for potential acquirees, including:

- Why and what is the company acquiring? What are the drivers for acquisitions? Is the strategy purely a back-fill strategy to bolster and bulk up existing lines of business, or are the planned acquisitions strategic and part of board-backed new initiatives and expansion plans?
- Culture and values—what is it really like operating inside the buyer client? Is the organization entrepreneurial and flexible, or regimented and tightly constrained by established processes and procedures? Are high performers recognized and given plenty of rope, or are they subject to close supervision and constraints?
- Remuneration and incentives—how are people remunerated and given incentives besides their agreed salaries? How are bonuses calculated? Are remuneration plans capped? Are equity-based incentives available, and, if so, to what level in the organization?

- Organization structure—where will the acquired entity fit into the corporate structure? To whom will the acquired executives report?
- Integration policy—does the company subscribe to short, sharp, integration processes, or does it run acquired businesses on a non-integrated, or partially integrated basis? Will there be redundancies, and at what level in the acquired organization will integration redundancies be likely?
- Road map—what is the company road map in reasonably specific terms? Where is the future? What key plans are being implemented? What part will acquisitions play in the future road map?
- Financials—is the acquiring company safe and solid financially? Typically, acquisition targets are interested in the short-term financial condition of the acquirer, as in will I be paid? But second level executives and other staff will be interested to understand the fragility or solidarity of the acquiring company. A few key bullet points can quell concerns.
- Who are the acquiring company's customers? Will I be able to sell my products and services to the customer base and generate income in the process?
- In simple and concise terms, what are the lines of business of the acquirer? Where will the acquired business fit in the structure?
- Human resources policies—if the acquirer has established human resources policies, what are the highlights? I remember when I joined IBM. Way back then, I was most impressed that IBM held sacred an open-door policy—even if, in reality, the open door potentially led to the street.

By making an effort to provide relevant information to an acquiree, an acquisition transaction can be de-risked. Of course, whatever information is provided needs to be truthful and real. Camouflage to trap acquirees will probably be detected, and create a worse impression than no information.

Mandate from the Top

Buy-side enterprises develop inorganic growth strategies at various levels at, or near, the top. Second-level managers may pine to acquire a competitor to remove them from the field of play, overcome inorganic growth budget challenges, or give them respite from the boredom of the day-to-day monotony.

Real inorganic growth programs need to come from the top of the organization—the owner or the CEO with board backing. Typically, the CEO in a mid- to large-size organization will have time to devote to inorganic growth strategy formulation, but not to the many steps along the way to a transaction. CEOs will typically delegate management of an acquisitions program to a staff executive to execute, usually the head of strategy, the CFO or the head of business development. Delegation is good, but only if the CEO maintains constant surveillance of the program, and insists that the pedal be kept to the metal.

An essential precursor to an effective program is a deep massaging of the corporate intellectual capital to establish a strategy. Merely bulking up existing—possibly decaying—business streams requires little strategic thinking. Thoroughly assessing new growth opportunities, with a view to acquiring into new sectors by transacting with high-growth rising stars is a more demanding exercise. But the large sector leaders subject themselves to this type of demanding process, and come up with answers. Smaller, entrepreneurial enterprises demonstrate this capacity and regularly white board possibilities and shoot the breeze. These styles of organizations seem to have the capacity to explore possibilities without pain or threat to egos or careers.

To effectively delegate responsibility for an acquisitions program, a very clear mandate needs to be delegated to the responsible executive. Target templates, valuation metrics, program schedule and transaction review, and approval processes need to be formally agreed and documented. Some CEOs will make the error of sending delegees and advisors off on a mission impossible. Templates that extremely tightly define target characteristics, valuation metrics that can't meet the market, and impossibly tight schedules don't inspire the execution team, but rather create FUD (fear, uncertainty, and doubt). Execution teams soon find that they have been set up, and momentum and motivation are lost.

One CEO I dealt with on several occasions makes it clear to his execution team that the acquisition program may be a career-bending exercise—a game of snakes and ladders. Teams that achieve the impossible will rise on a ladder, and teams that fail to achieve the impossible will be bitten by the corporate snake. Every step on the program is filled with FUD. When and if a target is engaged, the CEO makes it clear that any pricing proposition put forward by the execution team will, by definition, be folly and pandering to the unrealistic expectations of the vender. Every program this CEO has inspired has failed to produce any outcome, and has wasted the time and energies of all involved.

What this particular CEO is about is creating an impression with the board that a vibrant acquisitions program is in place, as instructed, while at the same time largely ensuring no transaction will occur. This CEO regards acquisitions as the reefs on which CEO careers founder.

When the board expresses its displeasure at the lack of results, the CEO hands up the heads of the execution team on a silver platter. He then heaves a sigh of relief and waits for the board to raise the issue again—hopefully at a distant date, and possibly after he has moved on to greener fields.

Commitment and Determination

Overzealous guidance from the top on acquisitions can be value excretive. Determination to transact at any price usually results in over-payment and at worst, if adequate due diligence has been confined to the too-hard basket, a handful of dust.

However, acquisition by consensus, and with the prime stakeholder (owner, CEO, head of business development etc) taking a diminutive role, normally results in no transaction.

Chapter 5: Buy-side Transactions

Acquisitions, in the final analysis, rely on judgment and a decision to transact from the top. Models can be developed that address valuation, typically by calculating a present value of projected free cash flow. Comparables can be gathered, but comparables are rarely truly comparable, with every business being different. Synergies can be assessed and post-transaction integration savings can be calculated and cranked into the model. Transaction structures can be developed that mitigate identified risks, including earn outs etc.

But, in the life cycle of each transaction, there comes a point where someone makes a seasoned judgment to transact or not.

A seasoned judgment is based on complex, multi-dimensional matrices of perceived risks and returns.

It is quite normal to develop a list of transaction risks and downsides. And it is equally normal to develop a list of transaction opportunities and upsides, and some detail of the contingencies on which the upsides and downsides are based.

Many CEOs are fundamentally transaction-averse. Transactions create risk and have career-bending potentials. Armed with a suitably extensive list of transaction risks and downsides, and some (very) conservative valuation models excluding any synergies and post-transaction integration savings, a transaction-averse CEO can persuade the board that a transaction is perilous in the extreme. Of course, if the board tells the CEO to transact, and at a higher valuation than the models and (selected) comparables portray, the board assumes the risk and the CEO is protected from any adverse outcome.

A transaction-averse CEO can use even more subtle techniques to deflect a transaction. Being rude and abrasive in meetings with targets, making it clear that heads will roll in the acquiree organization post transaction, pouring cold water on a potential acquiree's plans and projections, and being obstinate and negative usually does the trick. This type of behaviour is rarely apparent to a board or other important stakeholder.

Other useful techniques for transaction extermination include:

- Starting negotiations at a price point, and payment terms, that verge on the ridiculous. In one recent round of negotiations with a target, our buy-side client (to our surprise) uttered a goodwill valuation of about $3 million. This, subsequently over numerous meetings held over numerous months, expanded to about $12 million. By this stage, the target/vender regarded any valuation indication as a moveable feast.
- Going slow on the transaction process. After about six months, most targets lose interest and walk away.
- Extensively investigating minutiae in due diligence usually frustrates targets to the point of abandoning negotiations. Trawling through inventories, fixed assets, logistics, and systems takes a great deal of time, and—apart from glaringly obvious issues—rarely generates material value in deal negotiations.

Vision or Utility

To me, vision conjures up hallucinatory substance abuse, religious zealotry, and other non-commercial fancies.

But utility is a term that comes to mind, and which has relevance to all buy-side work. By utility I mean economic utility. Leaving aside all of the non-quantitative aspects of a transaction, deal or no deal usually comes down to perceived utility of ownership—which may be the same or dramatically different from the buyer's and seller's perspectives.

The economic utility of ownership of any business, stresses and strains aside, is fundamentally the utility of the after-tax cash yield produced by the business into the bank account of the owner.

I should hasten to add that not all business owners are economic rationalists, and often emotive or non-quantitative factors drive deal or no deal decisions by venders.

In a perfect world, with economic rationality on both sides of a transaction, it can be argued that no transactions will ever result, because the utility perceptions and assessments will be very similar, if not the same. In this case, no transactions can be executed unless non-quantitative factors become transaction drivers.

Say the board of the listed ABC Company receives an offer from the board of listed BCE Company (or increasingly until recently the XYZ Private Equity Galleon with the skull and cross bones on the mast head) and, of course, the price reflects a premium to the ABC Company's share price. A suitably prominent bulge bracket bank is engaged by the ABC company to mount a defense to the BCE company's bid, which is I-banker code for rushing around trying to winkle out a better bid from another party. If BCE's bid is scrip, or part scrip, then the advisor tries to winkle out an all-cash bid for a higher value. With suitable commentary on the front page of the AFR, the original bid prevails, or a higher bid is obtained, and everyone goes to lunch after fees have been settled. A good game all around.

What has almost certainly occurred in the case of a better bid being obtained, or in the case of the original bid being reluctantly recommended to shareholders, with the protection of a suitably letter-headed fairness opinion report, is arguably that the buyer has paid too much.

But have they?

What may have occurred is that the buyer has come up with a higher utility perception for ownership of ABC's assets. So in the hands of the buyer, the buyer sees higher value from the asset than the current owners perceive—and higher than the market perception of utility, which is what generated the ABC company listing share price immediately before the BCE company's initial bid.

Differences in utility perception are really what drive transactions.

The recent private equity bid for Qantas is a prime example of marked differences in utility perceptions. The PE players worked hard to come up with a game plan that materially enhanced the utility of the Qantas asset post transaction. After a long, hard, and expensive struggle, the pesky Qantas board and management have now got religion and are implementing many of the initiatives that Airline Partners developed. Of course, shareholder value creation will be subject to execution risk. Having the game plan is one thing, executing it is quite another.

While I have used public market transactions for clarity of illustration, the scenario is equivalent in the unlisted transactions market.

Where, like Airline Partners, a buyer builds a clever and executable post-transaction strategy for the acquired asset, the buyer can afford to pay more, while still obtaining a value accretive outcome. Mr. Murdoch's escalating bids for the Wall Street Journal illustrate the point—maybe.

If a buyer sees no more utility in a target than the current owner or owners, a transaction is unlikely, unless non-quantitative factors drive the seller. So informed buyers spend time, effort, and even money to evolve game plans that reasonably, without unacceptable execution risk, can drive more value and utility. Many factors can be worked into post-transaction game plans. Most of these factors involve the targets intellectual property, cross selling the buyers products and services into the vender's client base, taking the vender's products and services into new markets where the buyer has established channels and infrastructure, or even adding sales capacity where a vender has been short on cash resources. Increasing prices for a vender's products and services, reducing overheads, improving productivity, and many other levers are potentially available to the buyer.

The point I am making here is that transactions don't happen unless someone thinks hard and creatively about what can be done with an acquired business. All of the clever ideas a buyer may evolve certainly don't need to be transmitted to the vender, but the buyer's appetite, and the economic price the buyer can pay, will be directly proportional to the level of value the buyer is confident they can add to the acquiree.

Strategy

In previous sections, I have mentioned the issue of acquisition strategy. Operating management will usually evolve acquisition strategies that are fundamentally based on feeding on competitors to improve existing lines of business.

Chapter 5: Buy-side Transactions

Back filling sound, existing businesses by acquiring more product or services volume, more intellectual capital, more revenue, and higher earnings are fine and proper pursuits. But, let's take the case of an enterprise engaged in a really awful doomsday business, selling into a commoditized market, where prices erode regularly and the enterprise cops pressure from both sides of the value chain. Customers want to pay less, and do, and upstream suppliers want to provide less margin, and do. To make the same gross margin dollars next year as last year requires more revenue, more working capital, and more and more effort.

In these types of organizations, CEOs and owners need to look over their immediate horizons. If the enterprise is engaged, say, in selling PCs and other related gizmos, which are truly commoditized, the question is what can be acquired that will take the enterprise into greener fields? Now the basic rule of commerce applies—what you deeply understand is full of difficulties and pressures; what you know little about is resplendent with opportunities and rich harvest, until you really get to understand it!

But allowing for the above rule, there must be better pursuits and opportunities for growth in revenue and earnings than digging your enterprise more deeply into an unproductive sector. Most companies will reasonably argue that any new acquired business must have some points of leverage from and to an existing business—or you may as well sell up and start afresh. Which, in the PC box and gizmos flogging business, may be a better option.

But even in the PC and gizmos sector, there are avenues available for synergistic acquisitions that have the potential for greater rates of return on funds employed. Driving new services through existing distribution channels, moving into value-adding services, introducing related but differentiated products, providing education and training services are all potential greener fields.

In advising our clients on acquisitions, we always try to focus the client on options. In the early stages of each buy-side engagement, we mention the carpenter's rule—measure three times, cut once. Get the strategy piece right, and the execution piece is greatly facilitated.

Pace

Particularly in making unsolicited approaches to targets, pace is a critical factor. Playing a dead hand rarely works, other than with desperate sellers, in which case what is available to buy may be rapidly decaying.

Some acquirers will insist that the pace of a transaction be tailored to their time availability, convenience, and mood. If an advisor is engaged, internal or external, the advisor can do the heavy lifting without day-to-day reliance on the principal buyer. The principal can become involved at critical points, but allow the advisor to work with the pace necessary to nail a transaction.

Some principals will intentionally try to slow the pace of activities with targets, believing that deliberate and slow progress will minimize risk and get the best deal. Quite the reverse is more often the case—again, particularly in the case of proactive buy-side programs, and unsolicited approaches to targets. A slow pace in acquisitions is analogous to using slow tactics in a football game. Slow pace may be recommended in a chess game, such as the rules allow, but slow-paced football teams finish up on the bottom of the leader board. Slow-paced acquirers mostly don't get to completion.

Arguments for slow pace include:

- Makes it clear to the target that the buyer is in control. Some buyer principals will even go to the extent of running silent for days or weeks, to give the target the impression that their appetite for a transaction is low. The effect most often is that the target becomes frustrated, assumes there is little interest, and either withdraws from the discussion or maybe appoints an advisor to make some proactive approaches to other potential buyers.
- Makes it clear to targets that the buyer's interest is moderate at most. This is intended to send shivers down the spine of the prospective vender, and facilitate bargains. What this approach tends to signal is that a transaction is unlikely, and if concluded will probably be at a poor valuation, so best to decline and move on.

Chapter 5: Buy-side Transactions

- Thoroughness of process is facilitated by cautious and slow-paced transactions. We argue that thoroughness needs to be at the front and rear ends of transactions—the strategy piece and the activities following signing of a term sheet, including all flavours of due diligence, and transaction structuring. The rapid-paced pieces of transactions need to be from the point of engagement, through to the processes that initiate from signing of a term sheet—which could be expected to provide exclusivity to complete.
- Slow-paced progress can allow other better targets to arise, and the current target to be discarded. While I have heard this concept advanced, I can see no logic or merit in it. Targets can be engaged or discarded at any time up to completion of binding legal agreements.

Fast-paced processes on the other hand drive better outcomes.

- Targets really become swept up in the buyer's speed of execution. They tend to focus more strongly on meeting buyer's requests, and devote more time and attention to meeting deadlines and processes established by the buyer.
- A busy and rapid process tends to fend off any other buyer approaches during the transaction period. Most venders find it difficult to deal with multiple, very active buyers simultaneously, unless—and even if—they have advisors engaged.
- Speed of execution tends to create the impression of acceleration to completion. Targets taste the money, even though it may be only an apparition. A target's appetite and energy to complete a transaction are the buyer's friends.
- When a term sheet has been signed, and due diligence has been scoped and scheduled to meet the buyer's reasonable timing needs and comfort, off the back of a fast-paced process to that point, then in these circumstances targets tend to be more accommodating.

Attitude

People who have operated in the M&A business, as principals or advisors (in-house or out-of-house), recognize the importance of displayed attitude in dealings with targets. Novice buyers and advisors, full of self-importance and attitude, will set upon targets like banshees. This is a particularly popular pursuit in bulge bracket I-banks, and particularly with junior members of execution teams. They intend to have their way with targets, and seek to convey the message that any transaction proposed is driven by the buyer's pity and charity.

Rudeness, abrasiveness, deception, abrupt changes in course of play, derision of the target's business, and even personal abuse are not uncommon.

Being human beings—for the most part—targets react badly to these forms of attitude. At best they will be tolerated, and cursed out of meetings. At worst, their behaviour will result in disengagement by the prospective vender. Venders are particularly sensitive to process abuse, when demonstrated by principals of the buyer. Advisors detach from transactions when they complete, but the buyer principals lie in wait. If a vender, who has ministered to a business over an extended period and behaved like most bosses, perceives that life post-transaction—particularly during an earn out when he or she will be most vulnerable—will be detestable, they vote with their feet and exit the process.

In our buy-side engagements, we try hard to behave absolutely in the best interests of our buy-side client—but professionally, courteously, and honestly. This behaviour often produces jewels for our buy-side client. Targets will confide in us and express their aspirations and concerns, which can then be managed and fed into valuation models. We wait for completion and payment of our fee before getting our rocks off. It seems to work best.

Chapter 5: Buy-side Transactions

Digression #5 Wise Man

Beyond being an entrepreneur extraordinaire, Lionel Singer was a prankster. Examples of Lionel's pranks include:

Gary Jackson related an experience with Lionel early in Gary's days selling for Prime—Lionel's highly successful computer company. Gary received a call from Lionel. "Meet me in the park across from the Melbourne office tomorrow at 10.00 a.m. Don't be late." Gary was filled with trepidation—Lionel was known to be quick on the trigger and, at times, unforgiving. Gary sat on a bench in the park and Lionel arrived on time with a briefcase in hand.

"Gary," Lionel started, "I want to talk about your performance."

"Oh oh," thought Gary.

"Your performance has pleased me," Lionel went on." In fact, you have sold more Prime systems than anyone else in Prime—globally. You deserve recognition." Lionel handed the briefcase to Gary.

Gary, already thinking that a vinyl brief case was not exactly befitting such circumstances, grasped the case.

"Open it," Lionel declared.

Gary flipped the catches and raised the lid—the case was full of crisp Australian currency.

"Thank you, Gary," Lionel said and then departed.

I encountered Lionel at an industry dinner function I attended while working at Computer Power. Knowing Lionel passably well, I walked behind Lionel who was conversing with a lady—Lionel liked ladies—on his left. I tapped Lionel's shoulder and said, "Good evening Lionel, good to see you."

Lionel slowly turned from his conversation and faced me. "F---k off, c----t, can't you see I am conversing?" Lionel was having a nasty day.

After the sale of Lionel's IT enterprises, Lionel diverged into pyramid (not the computer company Gary Jackson ran and the Australian operations of which I sold to Fujitsu) selling. Having a global view, Lionel decided that Korea was the market, and NuSkin was the product. Lionel became a NuSkin dealer and unloaded NuSkin on his wide circle of Australian contacts. I grudgingly attended a NuSkin promotion run by Lionel to expand his pyramid, and arrived home with boxes of potions. Having gained rights to sell NuSkin in a Sydney territory, Lionel then moved swiftly to make market entry in Korea. Some months later, Lionel called me in a downer. Unfortunately, U.S.-headquartered NuSkin had also decided to make market entry in Korea and encountered Lionel flogging their potions in Korea with some "i"s undotted and "t"s uncrossed contractually, viz no rights to flog NuSkin other than in Sydney. That was the end of Lionel's adventures in pyramid marketing.

Another time, the phone rang late in the day. "Did you tell me you were going to Melbourne tomorrow?" Lionel asked.

"Yes Lionel," I answered. "I'm on a 6:00 a.m. flight, why?"

"Something has come up and I need to get a package to my Melbourne office urgently, by tomorrow," he replied.

"Oh yes, so what do you want me to do?" I asked.

"Well, you'll be traveling past my office on the way to the airport," he said. (I lived at Bayview on the Northern Beaches).

"Yes, Lionel, that's true," I responded.

"Well, I'll meet you outside my office at, say, 5:15 a.m. tomorrow, okay?" he asked.

I really didn't need a diversion at such an early hour, but I obliged.

Well, Lionel always simultaneously went in many directions when mobile. Lionel shimmied in a walk. As I approached his office block, I observed this small, heavily laden figure shimmying toward me. It was Lionel. Dressed in joggers and a Lurex tracksuit with short pants, he was something to behold. Sweating profusely Lionel handed me the urgent dossier, said thanks, and ambulated off into the early morning. Vintage Lionel. In an envelope attached to the package was a detailed note regarding the required delivery protocol and, of course, cash to cover the diversionary cab fare.

As Lionel was wont to do, he called me at home late one evening. "You must come with me to a meeting tomorrow at 10.00 a.m. Collect me from my office at 9.30 a.m. I am unable to tell you the purpose or nature of the meeting you will be attending, as this is extremely confidential. I will provide details in the car tomorrow."

"But, Lionel," I said, "it seems that I will inevitably know the nature of this matter when I attend the meeting tomorrow. Please fill me in."

"Well," said Lionel, "I can tell you this is huge, more in the car tomorrow."

Knowing Lionel's fondness for hyperbole, I assumed huge meant hugely difficult, but nevertheless, I duly collected him the next day. He directed me to a location in the eastern suburbs. We parked and took the lift to the meeting floor. We introduced ourselves to the receptionist—a well-stacked lass in her mid-teens, and awaited the prospective client.

It is not hyperbole to say Lionel was not a chap of height. The gent that emerged to greet us made Lionel look tall. The gent introduced himself as Dr. Iceman and insisted on taking us for a rapid tour of the facilities, which included several small offices with cigar smoke, IT devices, and, occasionally, people. Following the tour, which made me not at all the wiser as to what this enterprise did, Dr. Iceman suggested we adjourn to the boardroom. On entering the boardroom, which was decked out with samovars and other eastern European bric-a-brac, I spied a small—and I mean small—gent seated at the board table. He was counting what appeared to be suitcase loads of folding money. This was Dr. Iceman's way of presenting the balance sheet and illustrating the trading position of his enterprise—code-named Attention. Dr. Iceman explained that Attention was in the business of treating mens' erectile tissue challenges (viz an early equivalent of Viagra).

The gent at the table was introduced as Dr. Iceman's brother—but was surprisingly called Mr. Niceman. When the two entered Australia from their homeland in Eastern Europe, at different times and at different ports of entry, immigration was unable to quite decipher the pronunciation or spelling of their surnames, hence Iceman and Niceman.

From what little I can recall of this initial meeting, the profile of Attention was thus:

- Revenue—many, many millions—huge!
- EBIT—there is a lot of cash left over.
- Footprint—new service delivery points were opened weekly, or sometimes not, depending on how busy things got.
- Technology—the magic potion, which was injected into a man's parts, was shipped in forty-four-gallon drums from another brother (name unknown) based in Israel. It was then mixed in Dr. Iceman's garage, in accordance with a precise and exacting formula known only to Dr. Iceman.
- Transaction—sell it, quickly, to whoever has the money.
- Transaction value target—as much as you can get, quickly.
- Reasons for sale—Dr. Iceman was in the advanced planning stages for the launch of his technology into other geographies, and needed the readies for the new start-ups.

Dr. Iceman then suggested I meet with the Attention CEO—a nice and apparently rational young chap, whom I encountered subsequently in other transactions. I sat with the CEO and extracted some basic and admittedly unreliable financial information, and Attention certainly seemed viable, allowing for a revenue error of 50 percent and an OPEX error of 50 percent. The bank statement, presented in a flash and containing only a trifling portion of the accumulated shareholders' funds, caught my attention. My pre-engagement due diligence with the CEO identified one small glitch, which called into question a fundamental law of physics: What goes up doesn't always come down. Dr. Iceman was sometimes called to drain blood using a large caliber syringe from patients' members—priapism. No problem, happens only a few times a week.

I then met again with Dr. Iceman and his brother of a different name, and embarked on engagement mandate discussions. Dr. Iceman liked to cut to the chase and asked how much to get started. I named a monthly retainer and Dr. Iceman reverted to the treasury controller/brother who peeled off notes for three months worth of retainers, plus some expenses in advance, from the loot now assembled in $10,000 bundles on the board table.

Chapter 5: Buy-side Transactions

So off we went.

Knowing little of Attention's business sector, having personally had no requirements for service, I researched listed and private sector players. From initial contacts, I was able to excite a gentleman who represented some overseas high net worth investors (HNWI), based on the Isle of Man. This gentleman had dabbled with a listed biotech enterprise, made some money, and was looking for a new opportunity. I prepared a concise IM and started negotiations with the only active target—the HNWI representative.

Well-advanced in negotiations, I was called at home by Dr. Iceman at about 5.00 a.m. one morning. "Lou, Iceman here, get in here." Click. I met Dr. Iceman and his brother by another name at about 7.00 a.m. at Attention's corporate headquarters, with the CEO also in attendance.

"The shit has hit the fan," Dr Iceman explained. "The f----ing TGA is onto me. They say I can't import and mix up the chemicals. What a disaster. What a country. I thought Australians encouraged a fair go. Our deal will drop dead."

After due consideration, I took the Icemen/Nicemen duo to meet my lawyer, who brought in a biotech partner. After heavily accented discussions, the lawyers took on Attention as a client and managed to get the TGA to back off—for a while.

During the course of the negotiations, it came to pass that the HNWI chaps were in fact incarcerated in HM prison for materially naughty deeds, but continued to invest their not insignificant fortunes through the good offices of the gentleman with whom I was dealing. My mind dwelled on the form of action that may arise from breaches of vender warrantees.

It also came to pass that on a regular basis Dr. Iceman would ask for a private séance with the HNWI representative. Strangely, each such meeting resulted in the transaction value being pruned. "No matter," Dr. Iceman would declare, "they are nice guys and I want to do the deal with them. There is no other buyer—close the deal."

The CEO much later explained to me that the apparent transaction value—on which my success fee was based—was in fact only the onshore component of the consideration. What and where the rest of the consideration was vested I do not know, or at this stage care.

In due course, the sale and purchase agreements were drawn up and signed, and the good Dr. Iceman and his brother by a different name departed Attention's facilities. The completion of the transaction was followed, I heard from Lionel, by a mass walkout of Attention's medical staff who then started their own enterprise, generally with clinics next door to Attention's facilities. Lionel delivered my transaction fee cheque promptly after closing. I did not embarrass Lionel by asking indelicate questions.

What did I learn from this engagement?
- Cash is king.
- What goes up doesn't necessarily come down—without intervention.
- It is possible to make money from biotech enterprises without being subject to the diversions of an IPO.
- Leaders are born, not made.
- What's in a name?

Chapter 6
Sell-Side Transactions

For the purpose of the narrative, sell-side transactions include equity sales/capital raisings. The same principles apply.

Methodology

As with buy-side work, Newport relies on a robust methodology developed over nearly twenty years. The sell-side methodology has forty-three discrete steps, of which forty-three are crucial to the final outcome. Practitioners have, at various points in Newport's history, decided to short cut the methodology—tears before bedtime is invariably the result.

While every transaction has its own life and foibles, the methodology is robust and detailed, and proven over many, many transactions. The methodology is the backbone on which a transaction is managed through to successful completion—or failure for reasons that we can reliably diagnose by reference back to the diligence with which the various steps in the methodology were executed, or not.

Reasons for Sale

Each IM prepared by Newport Capital provides a reason for sale. Of course, we must rely on the client to explain their reason for sale, and then we make a judgment. Not all clients are completely up-front.

The various categories of sellers are outlined in an earlier chapter. Our favourite seller client is the one motivated by the realization of years of hard yards and risk; those spent in building a valuable and saleable business—show me the money. Our least favourite sellers are desperate sellers—their enterprises tend to be low-value propositions, and hard to shift. Of course there are exceptions. Illness, death of a principal, divorce, and other factors can generate desperation to divest, none of which necessarily reflect poorly on the sale enterprise.

Large corporates who determine an asset—an operating business—is no longer strategic or core are also favoured clients. These businesses tend to have reasonable valuation metrics, and the vagaries that often creep into private company sales mostly don't apply. Once the decision to divest is made, the decision tends to be immovable.

Buyers tend to look for a hidden reason for a sale. One buy-side client of Newport's always considers principals of private business to be desperate sellers. Most sales that Newport conducts are driven by simplex motivations—"show me the money" or "no longer core and surplus to requirements."

In the final analysis, the reasons for a sale are probably of relatively low importance. Proper investigation and assessment of the business will reveal the business's condition and prospects.

Various buy-side clients have an Irish view of sales if they are mandated to an advisor and are proactive. By Irish, I mean—"If the business is actively on the market, it must be flawed." Other buy-side clients display strong socialist leanings—"There is no way I am going to make these guys rich. Look how hard I work and how little I make and am worth," etc. This particular attitude always fascinates me—it contains its own explanation. I relish making clients rich beyond their expectations, which is sometimes tough.

Relentless Searches for the Premium Buyer

Newport has accumulated profiles of many buy-active targets, including past clients on both the buy side and the sell side. But the years have taught us that the premium buyer may not be obvious. So in every sell-side engagement, apart from notifying our off shore collaborators of the sale, and in addition to searching our own data base of active buyers, we always undertake fresh research to try to identify the premium buyer.

In the not too distant past, Telstra was considered to be the premium buyer of most Asia Pacific technology-focused enterprises. Some of the transaction eggs laid by Telstra brought tears to our eyes. The PCCW trans-

Chapter 6: Sell-Side Transactions

action in Asia, the (Sensis) purchase of Trading Post and Telstra's purchase of KAZ brought gasps or amazement and cheers from the M&A throng. Every sell-side client put Telstra at the top of his list—regardless of perceived transaction relevance. More recently, Francisco Partners' purchase of Mincom and TNZ's purchase of PowerTel elicited similar reactions from the M&A community.

Looking behind the scenes of these and similarly gutsy transactions, there are always some identifiable common drivers.

Bulge bracket I-banks advising large corporate buyers is always a good sign for venders. Not that I would claim all such bulge bracket I-banks are driven by fee maximization and therefore transaction value maximization considerations—perish the thought and wash my brain out for any such sour-grapes—driven thoughts! But at times I do wonder.

Directors of large corporates—and, in particular, non-execs—are sometimes accountable for what appear to be highly value excretive transactions. We have all heard stories of barroom encounters, or chairman's lounge encounters, that lead to value excretion.

Most of these transactions that are beyond the model and/or outside the comparables transactions are, in fact, driven by strategy gone wrong. A strategy is developed and advisors are engaged. Advisors ring some mates, or conduct a comprehensive market sector survey, and light upon a target of interest. The particular target is not in play, but after cranking up the valuation model, a number is produced and run up the flagpole. The target responds with disdain, and the advisor further tweaks the valuation model. The buyer client makes their enthusiasm known, and a feeding frenzy follows. Another jackpot is paid out and the valuation is melded in the buyers' books to ensure no trace of accountability remains—and everyone goes to lunch—or to a newly acquired villa in Tuscany. Bravo, well executed.

In our search for the premium buyer, we certainly take into account announced transactions, financially capable targets, targets in the client's sectors, and so on. But identification of the premium buyer is often more subtle. When we acted for Classic Blue in the sale to IBM, identification of IBM as a potential premium buyer was based on lengthy discussions with key executives within IBM. To understand IBM's interest required an understanding of IBM's established inorganic growth focus. While Newport can't be confidants of all potential buyers—even in a market place as small as Australia—we do talk with many, many organizations at a senior level, and we do update our CRM system, our data base of companies and contacts with extensive meeting and conversation notes, which documents particular zones of interest and focus.

The first rule in sale transactions is never stop targeting. I regularly find myself encouraging Newport's team to think outside the nine dots, and continue the process of target research. Targeting for sell-side projects is akin to mining. After days or weeks of frustration, suddenly a new target category will burst into life, yielding high interest levels. This is akin to striking a seam of gold, using the mining analogy. Boring deeper into the seam produces targets with a high yield. Targeting stops when a term sheet has been signed providing exclusivity and restraining the vender and advisor from further promotion of the sale, but only then. Without such restraint, Newport continues targeting up to the transaction completion.

Competitive Tension

Creating competitive tension is a subtle process. Declaring to an active buyer that they are only one of many targets expressing interest is dangerous. And, at times, worse still is declaring that multiple parties are undertaking due diligence. The perception that multiple parties are digging into the enterprise's innermost secrets, including client lists and IP details, tends to depreciate the asset.

On the other hand, even large, motivated buyers will respond positively if they believe that other buyers are active. Competitive tension can have positive effects on both the pace of the transaction, and on the achievable valuation. Some ways in which competitive tension can be fostered include:

- Sending a FAQ (Frequently Asked Questions) document to all active targets, in the interest of maintaining a level playing field.

The FAQ can make it apparent to a target that other targets are asking questions that they, themselves, have not raised. The FAQ can also be a vehicle for Aunt Sally questions to be raised and appropriately answered. (An "Aunt Sally" question is one that is asked when the asking party wants the answer to be enunciated, but already knows the answer.)
- Maintaining pressure for targets to adhere to the notified process and schedule, usually contained in the IM. If the advisor/vender does this, the implicit message is that something must be afoot. Moving swiftly to no outcome would be an unusual strategy. Maintaining transaction pace needs the active efforts of the vender—which are not always demonstrated.
- Sprinkling conversations with targets with incidental comments that imply, rather than state, that other targets are active tends to engender enthusiasm. Most targets take it as a positive that other parties are pursuing the vender. If targets gain the impression they are the only party in the process, the implication is that there are negatives yet to be discovered regarding the vender company.

Relationships, Brand, and Quality

Blasting out countless emails seeking parties to raise their hands and express deep interest in a sell-side opportunity is folly. The delete key is readily at hand. Placing entries onto Web sites proclaiming wide audiences with high net worth individuals is good for the Internet services providers, but little else. Most advertising we have done—and it was done only with a specific request from our client—attracts various unwanted approaches, mainly from people looking for employment.

When I am contemplating a major purchase, I have needs that must be fulfilled, but often are not. I want to feel that the opportunity is special and hasn't been shopped around to a wide audience. I would prefer to deal with a seller's agent that I know and believe to be credible. I want any questions I may have to be answered clearly, concisely, and promptly. And I would like an approach to be personalized and relevant to my areas of interest and my financial capacity.

Most particularly, I want to know that the party that approaches me on behalf of a vender is exclusively mandated to sell the asset. I don't want to deal with unmandated middlemen hoping to drum up a deal on the basis of an overheard conversation. I expect and want quality and integrity.

All of the above needs can only be met by long, hard yards spent establishing rules of engagement, methodologies, and relationships. Advisors are known and ranked on the basis of the quality of the opportunities they present, and the manner in which they present them. If I am fed a flow of rubbish, I'll act accordingly. If I am fed gold, I will await further contact and opportunities.

Strategic Fits

In preparing for target research, our methodology involves us in preparing statements of strategic fits. Fundamentally, we rigorously examine and hypothesize the likely characteristics that will enable a buyer to achieve maximum value from the acquisition of our client's enterprise. To do this effectively requires a sound working knowledge of the client's business sector (or sub-sector) and knowledge of how value can be leveraged by a buyer. The statement of strategic fits then produces a template of the premium buyer. Research can then be undertaken to match targets against the template. This is, in effect, the same methodology we apply on buy-side sector surveys, made more demanding by the lack of universal knowledge.

Figuring out the perfect strategic fit is not always based on pure logic. Relationships play an important part in the process. When Newport was mandated to sell Capitol Business Equipment some years back, I worked on the deal collaboratively with a practitioner (Dr. Chris Fay) who had an established relationship with Solution 6. In discussing strategic fits, Chris told me that a prime target was Solution 6. My view of Solution 6 was that it was an enterprise focused on the delivery and support of financial systems to the accounting trade. What I didn't know was that as we ap-

Chapter 6: Sell-Side Transactions

proached a balance date, Solution 6 was anticipating a significant revenue short-fall for the year. Capitol Business Equipment, owned by ex—Coldstream guard Derek Crosley, was the perfect solution for Solution 6. It was relatively inexpensive, a substantial revenue stream, able to be transacted quickly, and maybe even had some strategic fit—viz accountants buy business equipment! The transaction was promptly completed at a fair and reasonable valuation and Derek Crosley and his wife went on to other pursuits. No level of independent analysis would have identified Solution 6 as a high quality target.

Single focus enterprises are much easier to comprehend and assess as targets than large, multi-faceted organizations, particularly those that are rapidly evolving organically and inorganically. Figuring out a strategic fit with IBM, Oracle, Microsoft, Singtel, Telstra, H-P, or Fujitsu is tough. These types of organizations range over most sectors and sub-sectors of the tech industry, with many new technologies and businesses in incubation and research and development. On the one hand, in principle these types of organizations are fair game for almost any sell-side engagement imaginable within the tech space.

On the other hand, experience has taught us that it is imperative to first understand current hot spots; and, second, to know the organization structure and who to approach with respect to what. Making approaches to corporate M&A teams tends not to work very well. These people are finely focused on transactions in process, or high priority wish lists of the line of business executives. They tend not to think outside today's nine dots, nor for the most part are they intimately connected to the font of strategy development in terms of tomorrow's businesses priorities.

To gain ignition on a sell-side opportunity, we always need to initially be speaking with a line of business executives, and hit a nerve. While the transaction may well be passed on to corporate M&A for execution, the buyer is really the line of business executives—or sometimes the CEO if the opportunity is seen as very attractive and strategically important.

Tracking emerging interests and passions with potential buyers is arduous, even when sound relationships exist. Tracking the intellects and interests of the thousands of key stakeholders across the face of the tech sector is not feasible, even in a small market like Australia. But maintaining trusted dialogue with buy-active sector thought leaders is feasible and work in process, every day of the week.

Valuations—Art and Science

Learners—buyers, advisors, and sellers—want to cut to the chase and probe valuation expectations in very early conversations. Some more experienced players—like UXC, which has successfully acquired numerous companies—like to test valuation expectations to determine whether an opportunity will fit their relatively inflexible pricing and transaction structures. But even UXC is capable of a rush of blood to the corporate head, and pay full value for an asset they really want.

Naïve sellers typically mention need-based valuations. Need-based valuations are derived from an assessment of how much money is needed to secure the futures of the owners. We often find that need based valuations are based on the multiplication of a given amount of money by the number of shareholders involved. Five shareholders produces a valuation expectation of $5 million, $10 million, $20 million, or $50 million etc. Need-based valuations rarely get attention, unless the seller has the equivalent of the Holy Grail in its IP register. It does happen, but on only a few occasions.

At Newport, we have the advantage of highly educated, highly numerate young associates who enjoy constructing valuation models. The models, which are as meaty as those run by any of the large I-banks, basically calculate the present value of projected free cash flow, discounted at the buyers (assessed) WACC. However, there are various subjective elements in such models, and pure science is melded with art. Terminal values, selection of the appropriate WACC, determination of synergies and integration savings available to the buyer, and most of all the feasibility and viability of the underlying trading projections are all part art, part science.

Of course, most buyers will insist that all synergies and savings are to the buyer's account, and we regularly argue this case when acting on the buy side.

Our first rule is not to cap any valuation by stating an asking price. Our second rule is to establish—preferably in the mandate contract with the client—a clear understanding of the client's valuation expectations. If a valuation trigger—sell at the written offer valuation or pay our transaction fee—is not established in the mandate contract, valuation creep is likely from the seller client. The higher the valuations we secure, the more the client wants, etc. In establishing the valuation trigger, we use rule of thumb valuation techniques (EBIT multiples are the most common) that we can validate on the basis of other relevant sell-side engagements we have completed. Or, at times, we will prepare and run full-scale valuation models pre-engagement, and research recent comparable transactions to assess the client's expectations. These processes are important to us as advisors, making our living from successful transaction fees. But they are also important to prospective buyers, who want to know that we are providing properly based valuation advice to our seller client.

Achievable valuation on any unlisted asset sell-side engagement is very much dependent on the buyer's appetite. The classic case is where a large buyer, with extensive global sales and support channels, assesses a highly relevant IP-based opportunity. The seller, with limited infrastructure and cash, may be stretched to produce, say, $2 million of revenue. In the hands of the buyer, with all channels and guns blazing, the $2 million may turn to $200 million of revenue. Mr. William Gates is conversant with the benefits of tapping into a large-players established distribution and support channel—as is IBM. Of course, it is largely guesswork to fathom the likely leverage available to a buyer. But the level of leverage—and synergy savings—perceived by an astute buyer will certainly flavour the buyer's appetite, and that appetite level will flavour valuation discussions.

Typically, subject to the nature of the client's business, we will prepare valuation models (with full leverage and synergies as best we can determine them) for use in advanced discussions regarding valuation. Comparables are of interest, but real comparables are difficult to establish and tend to be reference points rather than valuation drivers. Most larger buyers will have run their own models, and we become engaged in a dueling models debate.

Larger listed organizations are more sophisticated in approaching valuation issues. Apart from modeling, comparables, and assessment of synergies and leverage, they will try to make every transaction value accretive in EPS terms. Some larger buyers—aided by their advisors—will transform EPS value excretive transactions into EPS value accretive transactions for the purpose of board presentations and announcements, by proclaiming that a transaction will be EPS value accretive in year x post transaction. This is cheating to get a transaction over the line based on the enthusiasm and appetite of the leadership team. Most of the followership team doesn't really get to vote, and probably doesn't fully understand the issues.

Other popular forms of transaction and valuation modeling include calculation of return on funds employed (purchase price plus working capital) and cash-on-cash payback periods.

In the final analysis, especially in regard to valuations of privately owned companies, a sale value will emerge from what buyers believe the business will be worth to them, based on their strategies, synergies, and leverage points.

Pace

As with buy-side engagements, pace is important in sell-side projects. The larger and more appetizing the transaction and seller, the more pace that can be applied.

Most IMs issued by established I-banks provide process and schedule details to be observed. Realistically, from the point at which IMs are issued, it is unrealistic to expect completion of a transaction in less than 120 days. Allowing for marketing and engagement processes, and allowing for back-end due diligence, legal documentation, and satisfaction of any agreed conditions precedent to completion, 120 days is tight. The work of the advisor is to herd the cats using best efforts to keep all active targets operating within the established processes and schedule. Most schedules are busy and material milestones can be established and scheduled along the way. Large prospective buyers with in-house M&A teams can be swift or slow, depending on what's on. Principals (owners and owner/drivers) tend to be even slower, having many other pressures and priorities to address.

In the first meetings with targets, it is always important to take the time to review the proscribed process and schedule for the transaction.

Sales Collateral

When acting for a buy-side client, we always relish extravagant sales documents—information memoranda (IM)—that make a Star Wars epic pale in comparison. Usually, we discard them, or sometimes make the point that despite the IM disclaimers (if such exist) we intend to make the IM a part of the disclosure documentation appended to the sale and purchase agreements. This produces the expected rapid back-peddling reactions.

When writing sales documentation, we endeavour to provide a comprehensive and fair view, to avoid litigation, lack of credulity, and horse laughs from recipients. We do always include comprehensive disclaimers, and also always include a risks section. Of course, the risks section of each IM includes risk mitigation commentary, which is useful sales material. At the same time, we always try to provide a fair view of the client's business. Performance hockey sticks and J-curve forecasts tend to be heavily discounted. The past performance is a material indication of likely future performance, but with some notable exceptions.

At the time of writing, we are mandated to sell an enterprise in the health informatics sector. The client has nailed several very important, enterprise-transforming deals and the past—as best we can determine after quite vociferous debates with our client—is a pale shadow of the short-term future. Our focus in this engagement is to establish proofs that incontrovertibly support the future forecasts. Proofs resonate with prospective buyers, if they are sound and objectively based on facts. Proofs are a long distance ahead of hopes and dreams.

In writing IMs, there is always the temptation to perfume the pig. We stop at the point of having clearly and objectively expressing the proofs and highlighting the leverageable assets. Surprisingly, many buyers have difficulty in identifying the full scope of potential leverage points and synergies. We try to identify these in unemotional language.

We also focus on providing pithy sales collateral. A 100-page document will typically sit on the recipient's credenza until filed in the garbage. A twenty-five-page document will possibly be read in a single sitting, and absorbed. We also try to work out how much highlighter will typically be applied to the document in a reading. If the highlighter content is low, the document is too puffy and needs to be improved. A sales document is intended to catch the interest and attention of a buyer, and not represent a set of matched volumes enunciating everything there is to know about the sale enterprise. The due diligence folders in the data room are the real sales collateral at the end of the day, and need special care and attention.

Confidentiality

Seller clients are typically paranoid about confidentiality—and we respect these fears. Of course, all material documentation issued to targets can be bound by confidentiality agreements, for what they are worth. We encounter leakage of sales processes from buyers and from clients.

Our advice to seller clients is typically to maintain absolute confidentiality and grit their teeth when and if leaks occur, or to tell the world that the enterprise has engaged advisors (hence the suits in the foyer) to arrange for a capital raising to ensure the enterprise captures the growth opportunities available. This is, in our view, a white lie, to the extent that not all sales are cash-on-the-barrel head deals.

Leakage can cause havoc. Clients can hear an enterprise is on the market, especially if predatory competitors foster rumours, sometimes driven by knowledge after having signed a non-disclosure agreement (NDA) and received an IM. This is dirty pool, and we encourage clients to have their lawyers send out very rude letters to offenders. Major suppliers can also pick up on rumours, particularly if they deal with multiple parties within a sector, which is normally the case. Concerned suppliers can ask very direct questions, and expect very direct answers. We leave this up to the client to judge.

The best advice we can provide to a seller client is to expect leakage and have a prepared script to deal with issues that may arise. The reality is somewhat different—Newport has managed sell-side projects over six months or more, with zero leakage. On announcement of transactions, staff and suppliers have reacted with amazement.

Renegade Buyers

Thankfully, renegade buyers are relatively rare. The renegade buyer will focus on cutting to the chase, opting out of the process and schedule, seeking exclusivity from day one, dealing directly with the client, and seeking to disintermediate client advisors.

When clients are transaction novices, particularly when set upon by a large and potentially high valuation buyer, they may succumb. Larger and more experienced clients refer renegade buyers to their advisor and shut down direct communications with the renegade organization.

In a transaction in the process of completing right now, as I type, a renegade buyer used his not-insignificant powers and standing to demand exclusivity and direct dealings with our client. The client made it very clear that the renegade was in effect opting out of the process, and was unlikely to be successful. Insistently, the renegade demanded an audience with the board, and was told in no uncertain terms that the board was too busy strategizing on how the sale proceeds would be used to engage in debates with the renegade. The renegade then reluctantly joined in our process, and submitted a best and final offer (BAFO) a few days later than the scheduled date. The BAFO trumped the next offer, which was the recommended offer. The renegade had lost so much credibility through its antics, that it was parked in waiting—subject to the selected offer completing, which it did.

In another notable case, a major telco worked hard to disintermediate Newport in a large sale engagement. The telco's M&A team told our client that they would not participate in any process being run by the client's advisor (Newport) and would only proceed with negotiations under an NDA of their crafting, which included an exclusivity provision. We advised the client to reject this NDA, but with the client imbued with the expectation of a quick, painless, and premium transaction, it succumbed. Three months later, the large telco had been embargoed from further acquisitions, and the client had wasted time and money. Competitive tension really is important.

Digression #6 The Banker

As C J Denis' sentimental bloke was oft inclined to comment, "I doff me lid"—to The Banker. "Doffing me lid" means taking off my hat in salute—C J Denis, author of the Sentimental Bloke, is a famous Australian author—from early 1900's.

I first met The Banker when I was dealing with a second cousin of mine, who was then CEO of a stunning shared services operation providing IT services to some major building societies, kind of a mini-Databank equivalent. At this stage, The Banker was a (or the) IBM mainframe computer operator.

While at Computer Resources, we made good business with this enterprise. We marketed the banking software in a fully bundled outsourcing package to financial services groups in Melbourne, Perth, Adelaide, and Brisbane; and made lots of money for our shareholders while having lots of fun. IBM watched, somewhat miffed. These deals were probably the first real, meaningful total outsourcing deals made in the Australian market. The hardware was used IBM kit, which IBM declared as being rust-prone etc. But IBM did take on maintenance contracts for our rusty gear, and waited for technology upgrades.

Chapter 6: Sell-Side Transactions

The Banker left the shared services operation, and became the CIO of a financial services operation. The Banker, being a man of vision, persuaded the financial services organization to fund the development—from scratch—of a new, all singing and dancing, banking system. The cost of development was to be recovered from sales of the package to other financial institutions—a formula admired by brave hearts. This paradigm was later repeated at Westpac—CS 90—and came close to bankrupting Westpac. The inevitable happened, and The Banker was encouraged to find other means of employment. A condition of The Banker's severance was a free copy of the software—not yet deployable, but well advanced.

The Banker established a new enterprise to develop the system and deploy it—mainly through managed services to second- and third-tier institutions. Funding was gathered from all available sources, including a high net worth individual (HNWI).

As The Banker's enterprise grew, with some notable successes, The Banker was subject to a palace coup, sponsored by the HNWI—who obviously saw dollars on his radar. The Banker put down the coup—with the aid of the staff and the staff superannuation fund—and proceeded along the golden road to glory.

As the enterprise grew and prospered—in revenue terms at least—The Banker approached me to raise capital for growth. Given the scarcity of venture capitalists in Australia at this time, at The Banker's request (viz insistence) I identified some U.S.-based potential investors, and off we went on a U.S. road show. Most of the investors we presented to—with The Banker doing a great job with some elaborate slides—knew little about banking systems and cared less—especially banking systems developed in the boondocks of Australia—which some confused with Austria. One notable U.S. banker remarked that we spoke very good English for native German speakers.

The one source in Australia that expressed interest was Macquarie. But the venture capital arm of Macquarie Bank (now Macquarie Group)—Macquarie Direct Investment—passed the opportunity on to the Macquarie IPO (initial public offering) team. We slaved to meet all of Macquarie's due diligence requests. The meeting was scheduled at The Banker's enterprise for Macquarie to present the underwriting agreements and negotiate final bibs and bobs.

I arrived at The Banker's facility well ahead of the Macquarie team, and cooled my heels (standard practice) for twenty minutes. I was then ushered into the boardroom where The Banker sat smoking a cigarette—as The Banker at this time was wont to do. Clearly, if his demeanor was any indicator, The Banker was not preoccupied with the Macquarie proposal.

The Macquarie team arrived chewing on iron bars, as Macquarie millionaires in the making are wont to do. The Banker left them to wait his pleasure and then had them ushered in. The Macquarie team flashed slides and The Banker continued to puff on his cigarettes, exhibiting little interest in the proceedings.

"So," says The Banker, "you want to make huge fees from an IPO? Well here's the thing. I don't need the money from the IPO."

This stopped the Macquarie team dead in their pitch. After some heated debate, with some rude words passing to and fro, the Macquarie team left the building.

"What the f---ck was that all about?" I asked The Banker.

The Banker drew deeply on his cigarette, allowing the smoke to drift from his lips in slow curls, and repeated, "I just don't need the money—and the fees were obscene."

At this juncture, I followed the Macquarie team and left the building, somewhat miffed that I had wasted countless hours on what turned out to be mission impossible.

Not more than three or four months later, following the rout of Macquarie at The Banker's pleasure, The Banker's CFO called me. "Can we meet urgently?" he asked.

"Why?" I inquired. "I can't make next month's payroll," he replied.

Oh dear!

The Banker's CFO and I met and the CFO provided comprehensive financials. It was true; the Banker's enterprise had negative working capital

Chapter 6: Sell-Side Transactions

and needed $5 million to $8 million pronto. I asked the CFO to take me immediately to The Banker, which he did.

"What's the story," I asked.

"Small miscalculation by the CFO—cash flow didn't flow, but a minor speed bump on the road to global dominance," The Banker replied.

"So, if I can raise you $5 million to $8 million pronto, on a pre-money of $x, you'll do the deal?" I inquired. "And you'll pay me fees of $z for my trouble and consternation?"

"Yes," said The Banker, "I may need the money."

"You do," the CFO chimed in.

My first call was to Macquarie Direct—Mike Traill, whom I knew well and highly regarded. Mike subsequently left the bank and went sane—he now runs an ethical investment fund—whatever that is. It made sense that all of the due diligence material prepared by the Macquarie IPO team only months previously would be a help in fast due diligence. One wrinkle, Macquarie asked Newport to act for Macquarie—they wanted me on their side in dealing with the idiosyncratic target. This was agreed and I confirmed arrangements with The Banker. The deal closed quite quickly, saving The Banker's bacon.

The Banker subsequently went on to an exit, finally, and is now released from his anguish. Macquarie made a profit and all was peaceful in the land. Newport's fees were paid promptly, and I think of The Banker fondly—but not often.

What did I learn from this journey with The Banker?

- Never, ever give up.
- Miracles can happen.
- Don't be preoccupied with speed bumps along the golden road to glory.

Chapter 7
Raising Capital In Australia

Funds can be sought from three classes of potential investors:
- Financial investors—venture capitalists and private equity firms, who are largely financially focused and are experts in all sectors and geographies, possibly including extraterrestrial geographies.
- Angel investors—in the United States, the angel market is or was responsible for more funding than all of the venture capitalists. Angels can hunt individually, or in packs, or can manifest in the form of family companies attached to very rich families—with or without professional managers to keep the plebs out of the vault.
- Strategic investors—such as IBM and Microsoft, who at times will make less than 100 percent—equity investments, but most often will seek a path to gain control or 100 percent—ownership.

The following text is focused almost entirely on the financial investors sector.

In the heady days preceding the dot.com bust and the tech wreck, I was told by a reputable U.S.-based venture capitalist that entrepreneurs raised capital in the United States by standing with sandwich boards extolling the merits of their enterprises on the corner outside 3000 Sandhill Road (the lair of many venture capitalists) and investors came rushing to cram their pockets with binding term sheets. This may have been slightly exaggerated. But based on Australian conditions in the late 1990s, not excessively.

Many of us will recall these times. Valuations based on revenue multiples, land grab strategies and IPOs of vaporware for huge raisings abounded. Australia was, to a degree, quarantined from the worst (best?) of this madness, but the virus certainly spread into the lucky country. If it smelled like an Internet play, then normal, fundamental valuation metrics went out the window.

After the Y2K rort had sucked huge sums out of most large corporations and government instrumentalities, and the dot-com bubble had burst, the industry went into atrophy—not decline. Unfortunately, the contagion spread into most sectors of the tech industry. Multiples plummeted; listed small cap companies shriveled on the vine, denied of access to further capital; and even large players encountered significant challenges and turbulence. At one stage, IBM appeared to be in need of intensive care and life support.

The sense in the tech markets was that the financial markets were handing out a very good hiding to all tech enterprises, for the sins and excesses of the late 1990s. The fact that the financial markets had inspired the madness seemed to be of little account.

In the period since the tech wreck of 2000/2001, the market remained dormant until about late 2004, when life signs could be detected. The years 2005 and 2006 saw some steady improvements, 2007 was a watershed year, and 2008 was initially a year of acceleration for tech mergers and acquisitions in Australia. By reports from Newport Capital's collaborators in Europe, the United States, and Asia, their markets also saw increasing M&A activity. The process of industry consolidation in most established tech market sub-sectors continued. By March 2008, the turbulence arising from the U.S. sub-prime fiasco, and the resulting credit crunch slowed down most buyers, including major, cashed-up global venders. Life signs are now returning as the listed tech companies start to regain their listing metrics, and buyers recognize that buying conditions are favourable, with pricing still below mid-2007 levels. What the balance of 2008 holds is anyone's guess.

Many of the smaller listed entities have reported significant earnings surges, and the tech sector food chain is again working, with end users spending decent portions of their turnovers on tech products and services. End-user spending is the fundamental driver of the tech sector.

Since 2000, most of the sources of capital for smaller entities have either transformed or evaporated.

Firms that were active in venture funding for earlier stage tech companies have mostly gone broke or transformed. Transformations typically involve the investment mandates being substantially broadened in terms of sector focus, and upgraded in terms of funds per investment. So the surviving Australian venture capital firms are now re-badged as private equity, and they manage hundreds of millions of dollars through to billions.

In the United States, in the boom, the angel investor market outstripped the formal venture capital market by multiples. In Australia, a few glimmers of activity such as Tin Shed (now fallen to ruin) and East Coast Angels (now flown off) arose. But the Australian angel (high net worth) market never became really organized. Today, the family companies punting on behalf of families such as the Libermans and the Smorgons have transformed and generally gone up market. A pity really, as the Liberman family appeared to do well from various tech investments such as RSVP—sold to Fairfax for more than $35 million. But of course, I'm not privy to their books, and I may have a rose-coloured view of their outcomes.

Various government schemes—invented by bureaucrats with substantial pre-approved travel budgets who went and learned from experiences in the United States, Israel, and other distant places—boomed in the late 1990s. Pre-seed funds, seed funds, BITS incubators, and IIFs all drank deeply from the Commonwealth's various troughs.

Most of the pre-seed and seed funds amounted to handfuls of dust. The BITS incubators mostly fell to bits. The BITS scheme was probably the most aberrant government-devised machine. Grants, yes grants, were handed out typically in $8-million lumps, for investment in (maximum) $400,000 licks. Some of the more enterprising incubators actually handed out the $400,000 with the left hand, and raised invoices for services provided to their incubatees with their right hands—as rapidly as possible. They invoiced up to the amount of their total investment, and more if the incubatee actually generated some cash from trading. Stand-out exceptions appear to be Divergent Capital in Sydney and In-tellinc in Hobart, with In-tellinc bolstered by Smart Island funds extracted from the Commonwealth.

Chapter 7: Raising Capital In Australia

The IIFs were less subject to creative activities. Some even really kicked goals. For example, AMWIN, a joint venture between Walden and Bill Ferris' Australian Mezzanine (AMIT), returned all of the investors' capital, the Commonwealth included, from its perspicacious investment in LookSmart. LookSmart looks less smart today—the smart dashed with the cash. This particular success had many fathers. Most of the rest of the IIF investees became orphans roaming in the capital-leeched Australian wilderness. AMWIN's early successes led on to CHAMP Ventures, now steered into less dangerous waters by Su-Ming Wong and his team, and shareholders in various less than techy enterprises such as Nudie Juices.

In the third quarter of 2007, sources of capital for small, early-stage tech enterprises are like the droppings from rocking horses—scarce in the extreme. A few brave angels still flap around, but few have the appetites or skills displayed by family entities such as Jagen, the Bori Liberman investor vehicle. Recently, The Commonwealth has again rolled the IIF dice, and bestowed four $20-million licenses, two of which appear to be ICT focused—Accede Capital and Prescient Ventures. Prescient is backed by $20 million from Jagen, $20 million from the Commonwealth, and is hunting for an additional $60 million. Starfish Ventures, John Dyson's operation in Melbourne, is one of the very few continuing, committed, and savvy early-stage ICT investors. Various others from earlier IIF and other Commonwealth initiatives preside over dead or dying portfolios, and I scan the press for good news from these residual punters.

The grave dysfunction in early commercialization stage funding for tech companies appears insoluble, partly due to the poor success rates of various attempts to tap this sector.

If we compare the Australian story with the results achieved in places like Israel, Sweden, and Ireland; the comparison is painful. There is a liturgy of common explanations of why Australian early-stage tech companies have not fared well. While the research and development Australian engine appears to be firing on all cylinders—within the various university aligned, government funded cooperative research centres (CRCs) and other enclaves of ingenuity—the outputs just don't appear to be there.

The liturgy of failure includes:
- Australia is too far from the major markets for our early stage enterprises to gain market access. Companies such as Infomedia and IR apparently haven't learned this, and have created substantial revenue sources in offshore markets. Networking events sponsored by Austrade, and Commonwealth-sponsored trade missions into various geographies fail to create traction for our tech entrepreneurs off shore.
- Australia is good at innovation, but poor at commercialization. This is somehow attributed to the DNA of Australian start-up managers. Again, numerous examples can be cited that make this argument appear spurious.
- In Australia, there is dysfunctionality between the research and development community and the greedy rascals who have the knowledge and skills necessary to grow enterprises from their research and development roots. The researchers research, and the entrepreneurs entrepreneur, but the twain appear not to meet. A classic case is Telstra Research Laboratories (TRL), now a pale shadow of its former self. Admittedly, TRL was established to examine technologies for possible deployment by Telstra rather than being a generator of IP for commercialization. Huge vaults of IP were created over many years, but very few outputs found their way into the commercial world. Telstra was typically jealous of other entities exploiting TRL IP, and most of the TRL IP was patented, wrapped, and stored on ice for the right opportunity to arise. A recent example of where TRL IP has found a market opportunity is the case of Firstwave Technology. Firstwave has licensed various IP from TRL to build world-class Internet and email security technology, but such examples are rare in deed.
- Australian investors find more attractive sectors for investment than the tech sector, notably resources (we are blessed with may mines), clean energy (we are blessed with abundant sunshine), wine (we were blessed with many Baby Boomers seeking new

life experiences in the vineyards, until the wine market tanked through over-supply), and tourism (where we are blessed with nice views and tasty, cheap seafood). This is the lucky country excuse, where it can be argued that digging it out of the ground, growing it, or showing it is far easier and less risky than inventing it and then trying to sell it. The argument then suggests that it is far better for Australians to focus on the use of technology to enhance the performance of our really important businesses, rather than trying to compete with countries not similarly blessed with opportunities for easier pursuits. If this is carried through to a logical conclusion, Australia will literally become a hole in the ground, surrounded by various agricultural pursuits, with people watching from the beaches and inland locations of scenic or cultural attraction. I suspect that we can do better.

Doing better is a question of will and leadership. Researchers will research, entrepreneurs will make deals where opportunities exist, but where are the leadership and national will to excel? In Israel, the chief scientist appears to be backed by a whole of government commitment will to excel in the key technology sectors. In Ireland, there has been a whole of government commitment to propel Ireland into the new world, fueled by the taint of past pain and anguish. In Finland, by a curious process of osmosis, the Finns have created Nokia, the world leader in mobile technology. Even Italy, famous for renaissances in various centuries and focused on various technologies, has spawned companies with global footprints such as Fiat, Alpha Romeo, and Olivetti. The Americans just excel in almost every sector they touch, from movies through to IT. In Australia, there appear to be very few votes in technology—and so lip service passes for commitment and leadership. Imagine if Australia committed to technology innovation to the same extent as our national will to excel at sport or horse racing.

Chapter 8
Miscellaneous Trivia & Minutiae

Advisors

In Australia, advisors range from one-man bands working with a mobile from their car office, to the large and powerful bulge bracket I-banks. Some one-man bands work their way up the food chain and others flee from the perils of the job. Newport rose from obscurity to a total head count of thirty-two in 2000, but sank with the tech wreck to a more modest five—then grew again in 2004 to the current compliment of nine.

Surprising to some, nine full-time heads in an Australian boutique is quite large—the equivalent of, say, thirty in the United Kingdom or a hundred in the United States. So, Newport must be doing something right.

Another standout is Caliburn. I first met one of the Caliburn founders—Ron Malek—when Ron worked as an assistant to Bill Beerworth and Malcolm Irving AO, at Beerworth & Partners. Ron assisted Malcolm and me when we sold a Tubemakers telephony business to Stead Denton at IPL Datron. Today, Caliburn has a very nice tower office in the central business district, with an appropriately daunting set of front doors, a sharp-edged culture, and a client base of major corporations. Caliburn dispenses financial rocket science to a willing client base, and reputably charges huge fees—a sure test of brand power fueled by intellectual capital.

Advisors at the top end of the market tend to be generalists. In a small market such as Australia, this is probably necessary and sensible. A broad, cross-sector focus enables avoidance of sector ups and downs, and the impact of events such as the tech wreck. The large generalists will argue that their superior levels of intellectual capital (viz really smart people) enable them to grasp the mysteries of all business sectors—from resources to retail, tech to teapots—and their high levels of unique IP allows transcendence and extreme value outcomes for clients.

Chapter 8: Miscellaneous Trivia & Minutiae

When we work at Newport for clients and engage with the bulge-bracket firms on tech transactions, we always come away with the sense that brand, culture, and posturing tend to be the lead assets used in engagements by the big guys. Divine levels of ego and self-importance also seem to play a part. I guess their clients think these guys can have their way with targets and their advisors.

In many of the lager advisory firms, their corporate finance (viz M&A) departments typically have some sectors on which they try to focus—including some apparently focused on tech. These firms range from tier-one accounting firms to law firms trying their hands at transactions to firms like Macquarie, where mastery of everything is synonymous with the brand value. True, Macquarie has people like David Standen and maybe others who have actual experience in tech businesses, but few large firms actually have professionals on staff who have extensive experience at the coal face in sectors where they play.

Several ground rules appear to apply in selecting advisors:

- Choose the person first, and the brand second. Choosing an advisor for an important business transaction is akin to choosing your surgeon. You want to be confident that the person you choose will chemically fit with you and your enterprise. Also make sure that the person you think you are engaging will be the person who actually does at least most of the work. Bulge-bracket firms tend to have their jewels on the front line for new client engagement discussions, but then the transaction is flick passed to associates wearing long socks and short pants, or the female equivalents. Few clients in SMBs have extensive transactional experience. The term trusted advisor is bandied around, but to travel the full gambit of a material transaction really does require good chemistry and strong bonds of trust between the client and the advisor. Every material transaction—buying, selling, or raising capital—encounters nodules of complexity and stress. This is where chemistry and trust come to the fore. Be sure that you can go to war with your chosen advisor.

- Choose an advisor with knowledge and a good track record in your business sector. In my view, nothing works quite as well, other factors being reasonably even, as having an advisor that has stood in your shoes and has an operating executive's understanding of your business, whether it be tech or tambourine manufacturing. Knowledge of a sector at the coal face brings with it established relationships, credibility, capacity to talk the sector talk, and capacity to present the transaction in the best light. Knowledge of a sector—and its various sub-sectors—enables the advisor to move quickly and confidently in preparing documentation, identifying targets, qualifying targets, estimating likely synergies, and de-risking the transaction and the transaction legal documentation.
- Choose a firm with credibility and reputation—which doesn't necessarily mean brand. Lofty downtown tower offices, high-security foyers with peep holes through which pre-meeting body language can be assessed, liveried butlers serving snacks from the cordon blue kitchens, scandalously attractive receptionists of model quality with suitable cleavages, etc., are all nice to have in principle, but they inevitably end up on your bill, which may or may not be worth it. The only real value to be assessed is the firm's capacity to get you what you want, and more. All of the paraphernalia in the world won't compensate for an advisor that lacks knowledge, has poor people skills, can't really sell, and has unsuitable chemistry.
- Be prepared to pay proper fees. Taking the least-cost option will probably deliver an advisor that is desperate for business, the equivalent of a surgeon with rusty knives and a pension for lunches. One-man bands will try to maximize retainer payments along the way, while some of the bulge-bracket firms will pass altogether on any retainer payments and really gouge on the transaction fee. A minimum team, for a simple engagement, must be a senior professional plus an associate or analyst. Teams will be scaled up

for large, complex engagements. It is not unusual at Newport for a team to consist of two senior professionals—to provide cover at all times—plus two associates. If you make an assessment of the direct labour costs involved over a typical transaction period of six months, with the team somewhere between 50 and 100 percent committed to your engagement, then double that estimate to cover overheads, then you have a starting point for assessment of fees. If there are no retainers payable, which increases the advisor's commercial risk, then you can multiply the labour and overheads sum by a risk factor. Over many engagements at Newport, we know that our direct labour cost for a small-scale engagement will be not less than $150,000. So, small transactions can be non-economic for the advisor and the client. The larger and fancier the firm, the higher the labour costs and overheads, and the larger the risk factor multiples demanded—even if they believe they have the transaction in the bag on day one.

- Choose an advisor with sales smarts. Selling a company, portraying a buyer as a splendid home for a target's life's work, or raising capital, is about selling. Strong presence, presentation skills, listening skills, questioning skills, negotiating skills, and intellectual horsepower, are all fundamentals to building a premium value transaction. Being really rude to targets, being abrasive, displaying ego and excessive hard-arsed-ness don't create good outcomes—for you, the client. And, of course, at the end of the day, the only true measure of an advisor's value is the quality of the transaction produced.

Advisory Fees

Advisory fees are a font of myths and legends. The lay perception, which in some cases may be absolutely accurate, is that mates meet over lunch, scribe a transaction on the back of a table napkin, agree on fees in multiples of millions over the last bottle of Grange, and head off for a late afternoon sail.

Oh that this was the case in Newport engagements.

Having never worked in the engine room of a bulge-bracket I-bank, Newport invented fees structures from ground zero. We quickly learned that clients are averse to some fee structures including:

- Hourly or daily fee rates, as charged by lawyers (viz blank-cheque arrangements). M&A transactions tend to be perfidious, and clients object to chalking up large daily rate fees when there may be no outcome—whether the transaction be on the buy or sell side.
- Retainer fees (plus transaction/success fees). Retainer fees are typically regarded as value excretive by the client, and represent risk. Newport is regularly asked—particularly by larger clients—to drop the r-word from fee discussions. They prefer we earn our reward from fully-at-risk transaction/success fees. This is, of course, somewhat raw in Newport's view, as the client alone can decide to transact, or not.
- Transaction/success fees, payable on completion is the only remaining option, other than various forms of reward from carried interest or options in capital raisings—such add-ons don't work on the buy side or the sell side. Of course, it helps considerably if the advisor has a friendly fund stationed up the hallway and can derive huge fees from selling a client to a captive fund, which has no objection to how much fee is payable and by whom on a sale, or a buy-side deal. Transaction/success fees tend to be sunshine at the time of an engagement, and tempests when the fee is calculated and due.

So, in essence, most prospective clients object to daily rate fees, retainers, and transaction/success fees—leaving only services for nix as the remaining—and strongly preferred—option.

In the face of competitors picking fee structures out of the ether, depending on who they are dealing with, Newport put time and effort into surveying the market—looking at fees charged by bulge-bracket I-banks, one-man bands, large accounting firms, and lawyers.

The result of this survey effort—apart from considerable confusion—was a fee structure based on—but rarely actually billing—daily fee rates for the staff involved. Each project is costed out/budgeted on the basis of staff member time estimates to completion of a transaction. This results in a value—say $300,000. We then negotiate monthly retainers/project management fees/milestone payments equal to upward of 25 percent of the total project fee budget—say, $75,000 on a $300,000 fee budget. This leaves an amount of $225,000 at risk, to be earned from a transaction/success fee.

Depending on the degree of difficulty we assess for the engagement actually completing, we add a risk margin to the at-risk component. At-risk margins can vary from a low of about 25 percent (for a certainty—which is rarer than the proverbial rocking horse droppings) to as much as 200 percent for a particularly tricky transaction. So the at-risk fee plus the risk margin may range from $225,000 plus 25 percent, which equals $281,250 to $225,000 plus 200 percent, which equals $675,000. On a $10-million transaction, the transaction/success fee can, on this basis, range from 2.81 percent to 6.75 percent. We don't rebate retainers against the transaction/success fees, as this is not consonant with the way in which the fee structure is worked up.

When we explain to prospective clients how a fee structure has been developed, people tend to cool down and recognize that there is some method to our madness.

So, if we agree to a fee structure based on the above formula, and we fail to complete the agreed transaction, at best we make 25 percent of our charge-out rates—and we have a really bad day. On the other hand, if we complete the agreed transaction, we make a reasonable risk margin on top of our charge-out rates. Seems fair and reasonable. Of course, when and if prospective clients object to risk margins, our retort is always to engage on daily rates, which becomes a circular argument from which we quickly tire.

Having executed many, many engagements of various types, and with widely varying risk profiles, we can quite accurately plan and budget fees for new engagements. When we open-book the plans and budgets, the typical reaction is one of shock and horror—people find it difficult to accept that a team of three people may spend half their time on a single project for six months or more. The reality is that M&A work—using effective methodologies—takes a large amount of time and resources. It's the nature of the thing.

Whether anyone else uses our pricing methodology is of no real interest to me. I go back to Don McCreery's dictum—good people produce good deals, good deals produce good money, good money attracts good people, etc. Or as Sir Peter Ables used to say, "Pay peanuts, get monkeys."

Management Meetings

In each transaction, buyers and investors will want to meet the management team of the seller or prospective investee. The standard agenda for these meetings is a round of how do you dos, followed by a pithy presentation by the seller or investee CEO or team, and then a question-and-answer session.

It's wise to road test each management meeting with a pretend audience, and a degree of formality befitting the real meeting. Using cooperative clients or past clients, industry cognoscenti, or Newport team members, I encourage clients to pitch and answer questions seeded into the audience. I try to seed hard questions that relate to the reality of the entity in question. At the conclusion of each road test, I ask the audience for frank and honest feedback—which sometimes causes grief.

Road testing management meetings takes the edge off nerves when the client appears for the real meeting, and provides insights—based on audience feedback—of the impact and effectiveness of the presentation and question and answer performance.

Seasoned performers enjoy pitching to any audience. But early stage teams with a technical focus find management-meeting pitches stressful. The key issues for management meetings include:

- Keep presentations to no more than twenty minutes—six or seven slides. People are progressively building resistance to PowerPoint.
- Listen carefully to questions and answer them concisely and honestly. If a question is a clear torpedo, take it on advisement.
- Don't volunteer answers to unasked questions.
- Always have a set of pertinent questions prepared to put to the other side, and make sure time is available for this important part of any pitch session. Role reversal helps level the playing field, and, if the questions have been well researched and considered, builds respect and helps with chemistry. Most buyers and investors like to talk about themselves and their enterprises.

Well-rehearsed pitches at management meetings are mostly on message. I am told by people who should know that a typical pitch meeting, at best, leaves the audience with about five big messages. In teacher training, I was told to, "tell them what you're going to tell them, then tell them, then tell them what you told them." This is a good recipe for management meetings, or all presentations for that matter, that need to convey some clear and memorable messages. Creating a large volume of noisy communication and delivering it at a frenetic pace is ineffective.

The most memorable management meeting I have ever attended rings sweetly in my memory. The seller's CEO/owner spoke slowly, carefully, proudly, and convincingly about his enterprise for about twenty minutes, without any slides, notes, or other aids. There were no questions. The transaction completed quickly.

Term Sheets

In-house M&A practitioners typically have the benefit (or liability) of in-house legal counsel. Let a lawyer near a term sheet, and the term sheet starts to look like a draft sale and purchase agreement. In the absence of in-house legal counsel, in-house M&A practitioners—particularly those with legal backgrounds—will be encouraged by management to expand term sheets to quasi—sale and purchase agreements, with a view to fully framing the deal for internal approvals and to save on legal drafting costs from external lawyers.

Term sheets however, are intended to be a means of capturing the essential terms of a transaction, and are generally non-binding (other than with regard to confidentiality and possibly other points) and are always subject to downstream approvals and events. So, I always treat a term sheet as a useful step in the transaction process, but not a step to turn into a full meal. In my view, apart from capturing essential terms, in simple and concise language, a term sheet needs to be quick and easy to prepare and negotiate. I have seen transactions stalled at term sheet stage due to zealous efforts to turn a term sheet into a quasi—sale and purchase agreement. Being non-binding documents, a term sheet should not be subject to detailed legal review—but rather be a handy template in the back pockets of M&A practitioners.

More esoteric term sheets can be developed to include various paraphernalia including:

- Break fees—particularly in the United States, or in other places in the case of public market and/or very large transactions, break fees are sometimes demanded by a buyer, and, less frequently, by a seller. A market maker may expect a break fee for putting a bid into the process, such that if their bid is gazumped they will recover costs and maybe make a yield for their efforts. This was the case, for example, in IBA Health's initial bid for iSoft, gazumped by Compugroup (Germany) and subsequently counter-gazumped by IBA. Framing the provisions of a break fee in a term sheet is a lengthy matter, and generally best avoided. Sellers can seek break fees, but the conditions that a buyer can reasonably demand tend to water down the value of the break fee provisions. For example, if I act for a buyer, I would insist that a break fee was subject to no material adverse change in the financial condition of the target

Chapter 8: Miscellaneous Trivia & Minutiae

from the date of the term sheet (with financials attached) as disclosed in due diligence, and the break fee payment then becomes judgmental—and potentially open to litigation.

- Exclusivity—buyers typically like exclusivity to complete enshrined in a term sheet. But, like break fees, there are many issues that emerge. Exclusivity in itself has various forms—exclusivity to complete a transaction as framed in a term sheet, restraint on the seller from further discussions with prospective buyers, restraint on the seller and the seller's advisor from further discussions with prospective buyers, etc. Generally, Newport advises seller clients to avoid exclusivity undertakings in term sheets unless there is a high probability (virtual certainty) that the buyer will complete the transaction. Of course, the buyer will seek various outs to completion, such as completion of full due diligence, satisfaction of conditions precedent to completion, necessary buyer approvals, statutory approvals required, etc. Some large buyers insist on incorporating an exclusivity provision in an NDA, which is, in my view, a complete nonsense for what I expect are obvious reasons.
- Scoping and schedule for due diligence—scoping the key elements and timing for due diligence as an attachment to a term sheet is a useful add-on, particularly if there is an agreed exclusivity to complete. If not included in the term sheet, then it is essential that the scope and schedule for formal due diligence is agreed in writing between the parties before due diligence commences. Due diligence can turn into expanding events unless an agreed scope and schedule are established before commencement. Scope and schedule can be amended subsequently if required and justified.
- The Material Adverse Change (MAC)—term sheets typically include a provision relating to MAC, with reference to representations made by the transacting entity. The material terms of the term sheet typically are based on trailing and projected financials,

and if these materially vary—or other nasties are found in due diligence—then the material terms will probably be re-negotiated.

Teasers

Newport Capital prepares one-page teasers for use in engagements (including buy-side engagements)—otherwise known as requests for expressions of interest (RFIs).

RFIs form the basis of initial approaches to targets—for all transaction types. RFIs can be emailed, posted, faxed, or sent by carrier pigeon, but also form an approach script for verbal and face-to-face approaches.

The RFI is a critical document. If the RFI fails to capture interest, regardless of how it is delivered, the game is probably lost.

In sending emails—the increasingly favoured form of approach, but not as effective as a telephone call or face-to-face meeting approach—it is critical that the covering email with the RFI attached particularizes the opportunity and presents a compelling value proposition to the target being approached. This, in turn, underlines the importance of the advisor having knowledge of the target to enable the opportunity to be mapped onto the target's particular hot spots of interest. Making an approach particularized to each target avoids the negative impression of green mail. Targets tend to dismiss approaches that feel like green mailings to large target bases. People like to feel special and are more inclined to react positively to approaches from advisors that know, and appear to understand, their particular interest and focus.

Contacts

Newport makes substantial efforts to ensure that initial contacts are made with the appropriate person within a target organization. Firing off RFIs by email to names picked from Web sites tends to produce poor results.

Of course, penetrating an organization to determine appropriate contacts by talking to personal assistants, switchboard operators, and names identified randomly is time consuming and frustrating. But, if there are no established research files profiling the target organization, and no established contacts and relationships, plugging away via the phone is about all that can be done—until the correct and empowered person is identified and contacted.

Within each target organization, there are only a few executives mandated to deal with inbound M&A opportunities. Most line executives are busy with day-to-day matters, and don't feel obligated to pass on inbound opportunities to the most appropriate person within their organization.

In large organizations with M&A operations, the M&A team will almost invariably be driven by line-of-business executives. If a line-of-business executive doesn't endorse an opportunity as being of interest, the M&A team tends to file the approach in the wastepaper basket. Delete is an easy option in today's spam-dominated inbound email flows.

This is particularly pertinent in the case of approaches to remote contacts. In Australian-based or operational organizations, it is relatively easy to establish an appropriate contact, except for companies such as Microsoft, which insist that all M&A approaches be lodged via a nameless and faceless Web site facility (black hole). But even in the case of Microsoft, with some perseverance, a line-of-business executive in Australia, or the regional operations, can be identified and approached. In large overseas-based organizations, it takes persistence and effort to establish the appropriate contact to whom an opportunity can best be presented.

I personally favour multiple approaches to a target. Depending on the nature of the opportunity, it may be viable to make initial approaches to the CEO, chairman, CFO, and CTO—particularly if the advisor has established relationships with multiple corporate contacts. But again, a green mail impression should be avoided.

Non-Binding Offers

Newport always seeks non-binding written offers "(NBOs)" in sell-side or capital-raising transactions. In capital raisings, particularly early-stage company raisings, beggars can't be choosers.

The primary purpose of NBOs is to form a basis for short listing of candidates for due diligence. Both sellers and buyers tend to be averse to hordes of prospective buyers or investors roaming around the due diligence materials. Due diligence materials include core, confidential materials, including IP materials. If these material are spread around the market, including disclosure to competitors, it tends to depreciate the value of the seller or prospective investee.

Newport always includes a template for NBOs in its transaction documentation material. Some parties oblige, others issue their own form of NBOs, and still others lodge only a verbal bid and refuse to commit in writing—a signal, of sorts, regarding the seriousness of intent.

Without written NBOs, advisors have difficulty in advising a client on who is serious and which bid, or bids, are superior. When Newport acts on the buy side, we encourage the client to submit an NBO if there is serious intent. Some buy-side clients are restrained from submitting NBOs—even with all of the standard caveats—due to internal policies and necessary approval processes.

Best and Final Offers (BAFOs)

Newport always calls for BAFOs in sell-side and capital-raising engagements. The facility of obtaining BAFOs is directly related to the market appeal of the client. If Newport has been able to create a feeding frenzy, BAFOs arrive; if the opportunity is only mildly interesting, BAFOs are much more difficult to solicit.

BAFOs need to be carefully prepared and detailed, hence Newport's rule of including BAFO templates in transaction documentation. BAFOs need to get into the granularity of the transaction—earn out structures, warrantees, withholding of consideration in support of warranties, balance sheet true-up periods for release of withheld consideration, etc.

Proper, detailed BAFOs enable advisors to provide clear assessments and advice to clients of the value of offers received, and can substantially aid in preparing first draft of the sales and purchase agreement. For these reasons, some large buyers prefer to hold their powder dry by refusing to issue a BAFO—with a view to continuing negotiations right to the wire—but with the downside exposure of being dropped out of the process.

Process and Schedule for Transaction

Newport always includes a Process and Schedule section in the transaction collateral. The Process and Schedule is frequently a tug of war between Newport and the client. Clients expect that all targets can respond in nanoseconds with NBOs, BAFOs, commitments to due diligence, scope and schedule, and other material elements of each transaction process.

Newport's experience is that clients create as much, if not more, delay in completing transactions, as targets.

Establishing a process and schedule for an intended transaction is not all upside for the advisor or the client. Hot opportunities facilitate, and are facilitated by, process and schedule documentation, and the advisor can use reasonably brutal methods in herding the cats along the established process and schedule path.

However, moderately appealing opportunities—or worse still, delicate opportunities—can necessitate recanting of notified schedule and process notifications, with obvious impacts on the target base. If no NBOs have been received by the scheduled date, or BAFOs fail to materialize, it is a delicate matter to re-engage targets in the face of a passed-in property. Sometimes, it is preferable to withdraw from the transaction process and try again later.

Assessment of Bids

Newport always includes, generally with good effect, the following section in the IM. The purpose of including the Assessment of Bids component in the IM is to create a level playing field for bidders by explaining how the various components of a bid will be treated in calculating the value of the consideration, in other words, how we came up with the true transaction price.

Basis of Evaluation of Offers—Sale Transactions: The IM provided to targets expressing interest in a client opportunity who have signed non-disclosure agreements (NDAs) receive the following section as an appendix to the IM:

All offers received by Newport Capital will be assessed in accordance with the following criteria:

Certainty of Completion:

Newport Capital will advise its client on the risks associated with completion, including:

- The bidder obtaining any necessary approvals for the proposed transaction. Such necessary approvals may include statutory approval, board approval, banker's approval, and other approvals to which an offer may be subject.
- Prima facie, an offeror, demonstrating that the offeror has the necessary funds available to complete a proposed transaction. Alternatively, an offeror will be expected to demonstrate that the offeror has access to necessary funding, by the provision of appropriate written evidence, to the reasonable satisfaction of Newport Capital as advisors to the vender.

- The level of commitment and appetite displayed by the bidder during the transaction process.
- The scope and duration of due diligence proposed by the offeror, which may mitigate against completion of the transaction.
- Any conditions precedent to completion that an offer may be subject to, and which may be dependent on approvals or actions by third parties, and which may be beyond the control of the offeror or the vender.
- The offeror being prepared to agree to a break fee payable to the vender in the event that the offeror fails to complete a transaction, which is seen as reducing the risk of completion.
- Any exclusivity to complete the proposed transaction, which the offeror seeks from the vender, which may result in other bidders losing interest or determining that the process is unacceptable for timing reasons, in the event that the offeror seeking exclusivity to complete the proposed transaction fails to complete the transaction for reasons beyond the control of the vender.

Speed of Completion

Offers that are subject to long lead times on projected transaction completion are deemed to have higher completion risks than offers that have short lead times to completion.

Newport Capital would expect a motivated offeror to pursue completion as a matter of urgency, but with prudence and allowing time for necessary due diligence.

Transaction Structure

Documentation prepared by Newport Capital on behalf of the vender will specify a preferred form of transaction (e.g. sale of all of the issued capital of the vender client entity). Offers that involve other transaction structures will generally be deemed higher risk transactions, as they may require various forms of approval from third parties, with such approvals being beyond the control of the vender.

Transaction Balance Sheet

Generally, Newport Capital will provide a transaction balance sheet, which may be a projected pro forma balance sheet on which the transaction consideration will be based, and on which agreed vender warranties may be issued.

Bidders should consider the proposed transaction balance sheet as a fundamental aspect of the valuation proposed for the intended transaction. Generally, the venders will not accept required material variations in the transaction balance sheet as notified.

Consideration Payable

Generally, Newport Capital will have received instructions to obtain the highest possible level of valuation and consideration for a transaction.

Cash transactions are capable of clear valuation at their face value. Scrip-based consideration should be subject to a discount factor, with the discount factor being based on perceived risk of achieving face-value liquidity. Scrip consideration subject to any escrow needs detailed analysis and assessment to determine appropriate valuation.

Deferred consideration—any element of the consideration payable that is deferred, but not contingent on any factors beyond the direct control of the vender—will be brought to present value using a market rate of discount.

Any deferred consideration—payment of which is in any way contingent on future events that are beyond their certain achievement, and/or are beyond the control of the vender, will be assessed as contingent consideration (see following).

Contingent consideration is consideration that may or may not become payable by the purchaser to the vender and is subject to future events that are beyond the direct control and achievement of the vender. This form of consideration includes earn outs and other performance-based consideration. Contingent consideration will be assessed as follows:

- If there is a guaranteed level of contingent consideration, payable unconditionally, then such consideration will be treated as deferred consideration, at the level of the guaranteed minimum.
- If there is no level of minimum payment associated with contingent consideration then the contingent consideration will be assessed as being of nil value to the vender.
- In some very case-specific circumstances, contingent consideration not subject to a minimum guarantee, may be assessed at a value. Such very cases-specific circumstances could include:
  - ➢ Consideration payable on future revenues where the vender has a very high level of confidence that the future revenue will arise, based on contracted future revenues that will arise for the purchaser, or where the

vender's sales funnel contains very highly qualified (virtually certain) future sales and revenues.
- Consideration payable on future revenues, where the purchaser can provide proof of virtual certainty of such revenues arising from highly qualified sales pipeline opportunities identified by the purchaser.
- The inclusion of consideration contingent on future revenues will be prudently discounted, to allow for factors under the control of a purchaser and not under the direct control of the vender post transaction completion (e.g., maintenance of required service levels, continuity of relationships based on individuals that may or may not remain employed by the purchaser, etc.).
- Contingent payments of consideration that are based on future earnings, and other criteria beyond the control of the vender post transactions, will be assessed at nil consideration value.
- Consideration withheld beyond the completion date of the transaction will be treated as deferred consideration, provided that the payment of such consideration is not contingent on any future event.
- Consideration proposed as being withheld by the purchaser and contingent on future events beyond the reasonable control of the vender will be treated as contingent consideration and assessed as being of nil value to the vender. Such contingent consideration will include consideration withheld by a purchaser in support of vender warranties—particularly if the payment of such future contingent amounts is largely or

solely at the discretion, and under the control, of the purchaser.

Other Factors

Non-monetary factors that the vender will assess and take into account in selecting a purchaser with which to pursue negotiations will include:
- The apparent appetite and enthusiasm displayed by a purchaser to complete a transaction at the terms proposed.
- The apparent capacity of a purchaser to provide a good working environment and career opportunities for the vender's staff.
- The apparent capacity of a purchaser to provide high levels of service and satisfaction to the vender's customers.
- The purchaser's intended further development of intellectual property of the vender.
- The good name and reputation of the purchaser.

The purposes served by the bid assessment material included above, and which is included as a section in each IM issued by Newport Capital as standard "boilerplate" material, include the following purposes:
- Some bidders submit wide ranges of valuation, particularly in NBOs. Wide valuation ranges typically signal intent at the bottom of the range. When it is made clear that the bottom of a quoted bid price range will be used for bid assessment purposes, bidders intending to submit a wide price range tend to think again.
- Contingent consideration based on future events—including revenues and earnings in earn outs—are always problematic. Lawyers can draft useful SPA provisions regarding contingent con-

sideration, but Newport always encounters issues regarding the inclusion of contingent consideration in the calculation of transaction/success fees payable on completion. Clients favour cash-out on cash-in fee payments. Newport typically counters that Newport's work is complete on transaction completion, and it is the client, not Newport, that elects to accept an offer involving up-side contingent consideration—and possibly rejecting an offer of higher cash on completion. As is typically the case with most advisors' mandate contracts, Newport Capital's mandate contract has a very explicit and non-negotiable provision that Newport Capital's Transaction/Success Fee will be payable on completion of the formal sale and purchase agreements by the parties, and that the Transaction Value used for calculation of the Transaction/Success Fee includes all initially payable, deferred and contingent consideration as defined in the Assessment of Bids component of the IM detailed above. Is this fair and reasonable? I say it is, because firstly Newport Capital's work is complete on signing of the formal transaction agreements, and secondly it is the client's sole prerogative to proceed with a transaction structure involving deferred and contingent consideration. Newport Capital advises, but the client decides.

- Deferred consideration—unless backed by supporting guarantees—may be deferred indefinitely. We have witnessed unpleasant situations where a buyer—and in some cases large and reputable buyers—have invented spurious reasons for non-payment of deferred (viz effectively vender finance) consideration. Where the buyer has pranged the acquired business through poor integration processes or bad and predatory management approaches, deferred consideration becomes a source of argumentation.

So the old adage of "What you don't receive on contract may never be received" is pertinent.

Chapter 8: Miscellaneous Trivia & Minutiae

Digression #7 Finglish

I have a high regard for a former high flyer in the tech sector who fell from grace as a result of the failure of a substantial enterprise of which he was one of the founders. The gent in question (code-named Blue Beard) would have been hailed as a hero in the United States and Europe, and certainly in Taiwan (where I have some personal, painful experience), where failure is regarded as a step along the path to success and greater fortune provided there was no fraud or manifest failure of reasonable governance standards in the debacle.

Blue Beard collected his remaining shekels, collected a few stars from his former team, and set about creating a vision splendid in the mobile content sector in a company code-named Finglish.

Continuing the relationship, I met with Blue Beard and his team in their office to shoot the breeze. Blue Beard told me of an acquisition target his team was keen to pursue. The company was based in Helsinki, Finland, and had developed core technology that was best of breed and crucial to Finglish's future success. I asked, out of curiosity, what steps were in process to secure the prize. Blue Beard explained that he had sent a letter expressing interest in the target company (code-named Ohio). Further, Ohio had appointed an advisor to execute a transaction. I read a copy of the letter sent by Finglish to Ohio's advisor, which expressed interest and gave some background on Finglish.

"So, what are the next steps?" I asked Blue Beard.

"Well," said Blue Beard. "We'll see what Ohio's advisor sends us and go from there."

"Sounds like a piss-poor plan," I advised. "If you really want to buy Ohio you should book a seat to Helsinki and set about negotiating a deal."

One thing always leads to another and, in December 2005, I found myself on a British Airways flight to Bangkok then a less salubrious FinAir flight from Bangkok through to Helsinki. I was accompanied by a Finglish director and had made arrangements with the Ohio advisor to meet his and the principal at the Ohio office in Helsinki at 900 hours on our arrival day. Uncertain of what to expect on arrival in Helsinki, I had packed my Herman Goering ankle-length leather coat and my Indiana Jones adventure hat—which both proved appropriate for the tasks that arose in Helsinki.

We arrived in Helsinki early on a Tuesday morning, with confirmed return flights to various destinations—me to Sydney—for the following Wednesday week departing at about 1600 hours. We caught a cab to the Holiday Inn near Ohio's office and were joined by Blue Beard and the Finglish finance director. On arrival we were told our rooms were not yet ready but we could shower and change in the spa, which we did. We obtained directions to Ohio's office and set out on a jet-lagged walk to Ohio.

To say Helsinki was crisp in early December would be like calling Singapore dry. The temperature was minus-15 degrees centigrade and, while it was not snowing, there was a constant downfall of light rain and sleet. My feet were the first part of my anatomy to freeze, shortly followed by my nose, ears, and hands.

Day one was spent doing how do you dos, establishing understandings, and gaining agreement to our proposed schedule. We intended to sign a binding term sheet by close of business on the following Tuesday, having completed due diligence and negotiations in the interim. This schedule speaks to my belief in pace in buy-side engagements. Ohio's advisor was helpful, and the key negotiator—a senior chap representing Ohio's investors (the founder—largely watered down from the 32 million Euros of investor funds drawn down to build Ohio's IP, including wastage)—was a large Finn with impeccable English (when it suited him) to whom I will refer to as Thor.

The team divided up the due diligence process, and by close of business on Friday we had all the data needed to draft a term sheet—which we did late on the Friday. With the draft term sheet emailed to Ohio, we took some R&R and went to sleep. Saturday involved face-to-face meetings with various players on the Ohio management team, picking up tips, and chatting to the Ohio advisor. Thor made various calls to Blue Beard to check on progress and talk up the Finglish valuation. Saturday night, we sampled the excellent Russian cuisine for which Helsinki is famous (but less famous than reindeer stakes, which I declined with due reverence to Santa), and on Sunday we went downtown to see the sights and have dinner in town. The outdoor market in the centre of Helsinki was in full swing on Sunday, and we all bought trinkets for loved ones. It was too cold for extended outdoor shopping.

Monday was the crunch day. Thor and the advisor set upon us like banshees, objecting to most words in the draft term sheet. I decided that Thor would play us right up to the deadline of our departure from the hotel, which was 1300 hours on the Wednesday, so adopted a firm line of argument. Ohio was stone-cold, motherless broke; the staff were all in disarray; most of the IP was of questionable ownership, and the few Ohio customers we had spoken with by phone were up in arms—I explained to Thor, again and again when Thor's English failed.

First to blink loses, we decided, so we stopped taking calls from Thor and the advisor. Blue Beard's phone rang late on the Tuesday afternoon—once turned on again—and sure enough Thor was on the line, indignant and feisty, but calmed to a degree. Blue Beard again explained that the most recent draft of the negotiated term sheet was the best Finglish would do, that we were all de-camping from the Holiday Inn at 1330 hours tomorrow, and if Thor had a superior deal in the offing—as claimed by the advisor with progressively reducing enthusiasm—then Thor should close that deal.

Thor advised Blue Beard that he needed approvals form Ohio investors in order to sign the term sheet, but that he'd see what he could do. Blue Beard wished Thor well, thanked him for his assistance, and said bye bye in the event that they didn't get to speak again before our team flew out of Helsinki, never to return without a signed term sheet in our baggage.

On Wednesday, Thor called Blue Beard about noon, to advise that he had investor approval to sign the term sheet, and that it would be delivered to the hotel by the Ohio CFO by no later than 1300 hours.

The Ohio CFO duly arrived, handed over the term sheet, explained that he had driven from his home somewhere inside the artic circle—Finns tend to live in the bush—and we shook hands and caught a cab to the airport.

I slept well on the FinAir flight to Bangkok, and again on the BA flight from Bangkok to Sydney.

Blue Beard and his team were delighted with the outcome and proceeded to complete detailed due diligence and prepare the SPA—with help from London-based lawyers. I did not need to return to Helsinki for the closing ceremony held the following April—but I did coach from the sidelines.

My reason for including this narrative in the text is that it illustrates some useful points made elsewhere:

- Never, ever give up.
- Pace is important in transactions.
- Term sheets can be useful aids.
- Try to set compelling events that govern completion dates—a fixed-flight booking from Helsinki worked for us.
- If you want to buy something, be proactive and as nice as possible under the adversarial circumstances. I received Christmas cards from both Thor and the advisor in 2006.

Chapter 9
I Told You So

For reasons that I hope have been self-evident in the text—including the diversionary expeditions and rambles—I have never been bored at Newport Capital, honing my skills, inventing my craft, teaching my colleagues, and dealing with all manner of people ranging from rascals and rogues, to nice people and the occasional genius.

The medical saying "hand of a woman, eye of an eagle, and heart of a lion" may seem overdoing it, but that's how I feel about M&A—particularly in a tech sector context.

The years have seen many arrive and depart Newport. Some lost heart in the tech wreck period, some found the craft—as proscribed by me and my insistence on methodologies and processes—too demanding, and others probably found me weird or a pain in the arse.

Some of my colleagues are genuinely missed—Peter Robson, Charlie Zoi, Ben Cardillo, Jay Hennock, Lindsay Boyle, Denis Gonseth (of HPI), Tim Ebbeck (now CEO of SAP), and others. They gave a great deal of themselves to Newport and contributed enormously to the growth and development of the enterprise. Some continue as Newport Capital shareholders. They are all out there somewhere, no doubt going from success to success. Peter Robson is making wine and farming snails I understand. Stuart Mitchell is now playing with bigger boys as CFO of Ironbridge Capital. No doubt Charlie Zoi is still testing his swordsmanship skills, somewhere between home at Sydney's Toaster, Queenstown, and his ancestral home in the United States. Alf Stamp works as CFO at Les Fallick's shop as principle advisory helping Les repel testy clients and count the spoils.

Regarding others, who will remain nameless, I hope their chooks have all died and their sexual organs have withered.

I look forward to another fascinating nineteen years at Newport, or to such time as God in Her wisdom allows me.

This is certainly the best, most stimulating, most rewarding, and most challenging fun an adult human can have with his (or her) clothes on.

About the Author

Louis (Lou) M. Richard is the managing director of Newport Capital Group, which he established in 1989 and developed into Australia's arguably stand-out M&A and advisory firm focused mainly on the technology markets.

After passing the Leaving Certificate at North Sydney Boys' High, Lou took up a Teachers' College Scholarship. He then graduated from college with credits and taught in NSW schools—working at Stuart House Preventorium school in his last two years of teaching. He studied for a bachelor of arts degree with majors in psychology, English, and economics—at the University of New England and Sydney University.

Lou joined IBM Australia as a data processing trainee, and was subsequently appointed operations manager of the IBM Sydney Data Centre. While at IBM, Lou attended various IBM internal IT systems and programming courses, and marketing training, which whet Lou's appetite for being a salesman.

Lou left IBM to pursue a sales career at Computer Resources Group, the largest indigenous Australian technology firm of its day, and became the Group CEO at the age of thirty-two. Lou left Computer Resources after an attempted management buyout (MBO), and teamed up with George Farley, a well-known Melbourne IT entrepreneur and technologist, to develop George's Melbourne-based software business into the highly successful Australian Technology & Computers (ATAC) Group. In 1985, the ATAC Group was split into its Sydney- and Melbourne-based operations, and Lou sold the Sydney-based operations to a United Kingdom acquirer. Lou became the Chairman of the U.K. group and worked in London from 1985 to 1987.

Returning to Sydney in 1987, Lou then took on extended consulting engagements—first with Computer Power Group as general manager—Business Development and subsequently with International Computers

Limited (ICL) Australia as Asia Pacific marketing director. Lou left ICL to establish Newport Capital Group in 1989.

Since leaving IBM, Lou's career has been heavily focused on M&A transactions and start-ups, most of which were successful. Lou's line management experience includes operations in most sectors of the ICT industry. Newport Capital is Lou's longest and happiest business engagement. Lou is passionate about assisting Australian ICT companies and entrepreneurs.

Lou is married to Kay, his wife of forty-two years, and has three children and four grandchildren. Lou lives at Balmoral Beach on Sydney's lower North Shore.